THE WAY WE KNOW IN DREAMS

ALSO BY GORDON WEAVER

Novels

Count a Lonely Cadence
Give Him a Stone
Circling Byzantium
The Eight Corners of the World

Story Collections

The Entombed Man of Thule
Such Waltzing Was Not Easy
Getting Serious
Morality Play
A World Quite Round
Men Who Would Be Good

THE WAY
WE KNOW
IN DREAMS

Stories by

GORDON WEAVER

UNIVERSITY OF MISSOURI PRESS

Columbia and London

Copyright © 1994 by Gordon Weaver
University of Missouri Press, Columbia, Missouri 65201
Printed and bound in the United States of America
All rights reserved
5 4 3 2 1   97 96 95 94 94

Library of Congress Cataloging-in-Publication Data
Weaver, Gordon.
    The way we know in dreams : stories / by Gordon Weaver.
        p.   cm.
    ISBN 0-8262-0931-9 (alk. paper)
    I. Title.
PS3573.E17W3   1994
813'.54—dc20   93-38323
                                                        CIP

♾™ This paper meets the requirements of the
American National Standard for Permanence of Paper
for Printed Library Materials, Z39.48, 1984.

Designer: Rhonda Miller
Typesetter: Connell-Zeko Type & Graphics
Printer and Binder: Thomson-Shore, Inc.
Typefaces: Berkeley Oldstyle and Aquiline

For credits, see the last printed page of this book.

for Judy, Kristina, Anna, Jessica

and for Dennis Shryack, faith and diligence
over the long haul—and for Jack Myers,
poet-*mensch* of the first order!

CONTENTS

THE WAY WE KNOW IN DREAMS

What kept me goggling all that hour? The nice
Discernment of a lime or lemon slice?
A hope of lewd espials? An astounded
Sense of the import of a thing surrounded—
Of what a Z or almond-leaf became
Within the sudden premise of a frame?
All these, and that my eye should flutter there,
By shrewd promotion, in the outstretched air,
An unseen genius of the middle distance,
Giddy with godhead or with nonexistence.

Richard Wilbur, "The Eye"

FEARING WHAT DREAMS?

இ

I take a seat on the cottage porch. I have gin, but no tonic, no ice cubes. I sit in my mother's huge fan-back wickerwork chair. I smoke many cigarettes.

The sunset is spectacular. The sun descends, yellow as a yolk, melts to dull gold as it subsides behind the horizon of the far shore. A rosy patina spreads like oil across the black surface of the lake. The breeze dies with the setting sun.

I have wound and set the old banjo clock on the wall. It runs, hums as though it had never stopped. I listen to the clock in the full dark of the night. When I move to pour another drink, lift the glass to my mouth, the wickerwork chair creaks and squeals loudly. Sitting very still, I hear the clock, my own breathing, the sporadic swish of traffic from the state highway. Summer people, vacationers, weekenders, heading south for home, Milwaukee, Chicago.

A fitful northwest wind rises. I shudder involuntarily, raise goose bumps on my bare arms. Before the night sky clouds over, I see this wind chop the surface of Silver Lake, stretching out below and beyond the bluff. Clouds conceal the rising moon, no broken shimmer of moonlight on the water, no stars in the night sky.

The shifting wind carries the sound of increased traffic from the highway. And music. I can hear music in the wind. Fragments of a band all the way from the east end of the lake, the last dance of the season at the Waushara Resort pavilion. From much closer, at the junction of the lake road and the state highway, the wind brings me the roll of jukebox music, like summer thunder, at Wally Weller's Moosehead Tavern.

When the wind gusts, the high boughs of the tall Norway pines surrounding the cottage sound like loud sighing. When the wind gusts strongly there are minute noises in the cottage, as if there were other people here with me, moving about the empty rooms.

When I strike a match, draw on my cigarette, there is light to show me myself sitting on the cottage porch, looking out at the darkness. There are still a few dock lights and lighted cottage windows across Silver Lake. They shine in the night like stars, then wink out, one by one. When I do not smoke, there is nothing to see.

As the night continues, it is colder. I hear the key-wind banjo clock humming efficiently. I hear the splash of gin I pour into my glass. I hear the steady traffic, cars, campers, trailers, going home, south, on the state highway. Until very late, I still hear bits of music carried on the wind to me from the Waushara Resort pavilion and Wally Weller's Moosehead Tavern. I do not listen for anything in particular.

I make up a bed for myself. At first I fear I will not be able to sleep. But I feel the gin I have been drinking, and the heavy quilt I snuggle under has a cozy tinge of dampness in it from long storage. My pillow has a delicious stale odor. Now I hear only the wind in the high pine boughs and the hum of the clock on the wall.

My last thought before I sleep is that I will dream. But I do not dream. Or, if I do, I have no memory of dreams when I wake, late in the morning. It is a sleep as fine and deep as any I have ever known.

Parker was too small to be any help. He watched while his grandfather dug the wide steps into the sandy clay soil. Parker

Fearing What Dreams?

stood back to one side on the slope to catch dapples of shade where the boughs waved a little in the last of the morning's lake breeze. There was no relief from the mid-day heat in the flitting spots of shade. It hurt his eyes to look at the brilliant surface of the lake, so he watched his grandfather work.

He was very strong. Cords stood out in his throat as he dug, set the creosoted railroad ties in to make each step, anchored them. Muscles rippled in his grandfather's arms, veins swelled in the backs of his mottled hands, sweat soaked his shirt in front and back, gathered like crystals in the hair of his forearms. Feeling useless, Parker needed to say something.

"Hard work," he said to his grandfather.

"I'll say," his grandfather said, and, "They last though. Be here even when you're long gone." Parker felt helpless, unable to think of anything to say.

"Well, Parker," I say to myself, to the cold air of late morning, "here you are." Leaning into the stiff, chill wind, I pace my lot line along the lake road, locate the corner. The stake has weathered away, but the cluster of small rocks shows flecks of red paint, applied by the surveyor at the time of my mother's death, when the property passed to me in her will.

The driveway, two dirt ruts partially overgrown by ferns that lean in toward the grassy crown, leads in from the lake road, past the storage barn my grandfather built for the cart and horse he kept for my grandmother's summer amusement. She liked to ride, once or twice a week, all the way round Silver Lake. I was told this by my father, who often accompanied her when he was a boy. She died many years before my birth.

My father stored his boats there in winter. It is padlocked, the key no doubt put safely away, forgotten, in the cottage. When my father pushed back the sliding door, opening for the season each Memorial Day, I used to stand by, imagine winter itself had been stored away inside with our boats. I imagined the last frozen mass of winter's substance tumbling out the open door to melt at my feet on the pine needles warm with soft spring sun. Daylight crept slowly inside as the door moved on its rusty track, as if it had to push into the cold darkness. There was always a rustling sound as we entered, my father and I, rodents scrambling for cover. Once, a large blacksnake whipped through the slice of light, slithering into a deeper, still-dark corner, like the soul of winter, in retreat.

I kick the door with the toe of my shoe, trying to sound the depths of the barn with the echo, but there is no echo out here in the steady wind.

Moving in toward the cottage, I skirt the cistern cover. This is a habit, taught me by my mother, who feared my death by drowning because she never learned to swim well.

I pass the tilted outhouse, stop, pry open the door. I remember when we moved it once, dug a new pit. The two-holer seat had been chewed—by beavers, my father said, or muskrats, seeking salts in the wood. It has no smell at all in this biting air. It was my chore as a boy to shake lime down the holes to keep away flies and stink. I never feared falling into the cistern but feared sitting in the outhouse, that something, snake or woodchuck, would bite my bottom. I cannot close the door properly. I cringe to think of using it through the winter.

My cottage looks abandoned, windows shuttered fast, cedar shake shingles aged to dull silver, clapboards grey, bare patches of wood weathered white where the paint has chipped and peeled. Home, Parker, I tell myself, is where you are.

The edge of the bluff gives me the panorama of Silver Lake. Wind moils the surface, strikes small, hard glints of the remote sun's cold reflection. To the west and north, there is an approaching cast in the sky. The pine trees take the wind fully as it whoops up from the bowl of the lake, swaying, trunks creaking, topmost boughs whispering loudly, shrieking. It is colder here, in the unceasing face of the wind.

I descend the wide steps set into the bluff. My beach is narrow, untended. The grassy slope has crawled a few feet into the sandy strip, and the sand, even near the water, is pocked with clumps of spiked grass. The rim of the lake, lapping the sand, is thick with seaweed.

The water is shallow for some distance from the shore. It is clear to the hard bottom, that bottom rippled, ridged by the perpetual currents, like the rungs of a ladder. I think of ladder rungs as I remember the feel of that ridged sand bottom on my bare feet as I entered the water, my mother watching over me from a canvas beach chair, her sunglasses and broad-brimmed hat.

I stop this. It is not what I am here for. Here, I tell myself. Not then, or later, or anywhere except here and now, this place and time. Parker, I say to myself, starting back up the steps in the slope, here you are. I do not speak aloud, to the lake or sky or trees. I have nothing more to say.

Parker helped as much as he could. While his father drove pier pilings into the sandy bottom of the lake with a maul, he carried buckets of water up the slope from the beach for his mother, poured for her while she primed the kitchen pump. The dry pump leathers sounded like the hoarse wheezing of an asthmatic. If he listened, he heard the echo of his father's driving maul, the dull smack like a canoe paddle slapping the surface of the lake.

He gathered pine cones and burned them in the big stone fireplace to evaporate the lingering damp of the long winter from the cottage walls. While his father climbed a ladder to clean the year's accumulation of pine needles from the gutters, Parker pulled shutter nails within his reach with the claw hammer. It was not hard, and he felt a necessary part of the work, the Memorial Day weather so fine, he had to say something to his father as they worked together to open the cottage for another season.

"This is real fun," Parker said.

"Yeah, and it's work too," his father said, "let's keep at it, shall we?"

It was the last moose, my father told me when I was a boy, shot south of Baraboo after the First World War. His father remembered the carcass strung up for display outside the post office in Wautoma, the head sent by milk train to a Chicago taxidermist, mounted by Wally Weller's father outside over the front door to his tavern. When my father was a boy he knew Wally Weller's father. The trophy frightened me when I was a child, holding my father's hand, come to drink soda and play the slot machine while he drank beer with Wally Weller. I thought it was still alive, saw menace in its trusting snout, sentience in its glaring glass eyeballs, danger in its massive rack.

"I'm closed, mister," Wally Weller says, "now until deer season starts."

"It's me, Wally, Parker. Parker," I say. "You mean I've changed so much you don't even recognize me?" The barroom is so dark I am momentarily blinded, eyes running tears from the cold wind. "You blotto already this early in the day? Parker," I say, thrust my hand out to him. He lets go his glass with reluctance, touches mine with a hand as lifelessly dry as paper. His father drank himself to death.

"The which?" says Wally. "Sure, Parker. What the hell you doing up here? You should of been here last night, Parker. Party, party," he says, moving his head as if there were still jukebox music, a crowd in the barroom.

"I came up from Chicago last night, Wally. I'm staying at the cottage for a while. I need to get some firewood. Can I use your phone? You should look outside, it's turned cold enough to freeze your wazoo off, Wally."

"Which?" says Wally. I begin to adjust to the dimness, surprised to see he has changed so little. His hair is dyed, a black so black it accentuates his sallow complexion, a gleam of oil on his hair, sheen of lotion on his cheeks and forehead and chin, his eyes moist, a rosy alcoholic's tint over his shining face. When he lifts his glass to drink, he must use both hands to control his tremor. The barroom is too warm, stuffy, the smell of his cologne like a woman's aura of perfume around him.

"Wally? Are you listening to me?"

"Parker," Wally Weller says, "you bring your wife and kiddies up here after Labor Day? Cold, man. Cold tonight. Could be snow. Believe it. Go home, Parker, take wife and kiddies home to Milwaukee."

"Chicago," I say. "When my folks were alive we lived in Milwaukee. You remember my father, Wally? My father knew your father. I moved to Chicago before I got married."

"Take wife and kiddies home, Parker," he says. "Come back next summer."

"They're home. In Chicago," I say. "Where's your phone, Wally?"

"Have a drinkie. No? You must be bats. Either you're a lush or you're bats. I'd be bats, you know, if it wasn't for I lush it."

"It's so stuffy in here. Why don't you open a window? Why do you keep the lights off?" I say.

"Labor Day, party, party," he says, stands on the rungs of his barstool, teeters, catches the edge of the bar for support, leans across the bar, lifts a bottle of vodka, sits, thumps the bottle down on the bar as if it were an official seal. "Lush," says Wally Weller. He pours vodka into the melting ice and dregs of his drink, drinks with both hands, smacks his lips dry. "You don't know from lushing. Where the hell you get off, Parker? You're snugged in with wife and kiddies all winter long. You got kiddies?"

"Two sons."

"God love you, Parker," he says with a sneer. "Pray for poor old Wally socked in here lushing it, Parker. I got to lush if I don't want to go bats, see. Sometime, remember old Wally here lushing it, okay? Oh, shit, man," Wally Weller says, begins to cry.

"Wally, can you remember when I was a kid? Remember my folks? My old man used to sit right here and drink beer with you. Could you possibly please stop crying, Wally?" I say. He speaks, but I cannot understand him. He cries, blubbers like a child, tears wetting his mouth and chin, babbling that he is a lush and must lush it, he thinks he will go bats this winter. I cannot see a telephone in the bar.

Wally Weller cries and cries, cannot lift his glass without spilling, slobbering. The room is so dark, so warm, the close stench of his cologne and hair oil, I breathe hard for air, choking. "Don't cry, Wally," I say, leave him, weeping, rush outside, close the door behind me, put my ear to it, do not hear him through the closed door, the whistling wind.

The mounted moosehead is a ruin. Its flared nostrils are plugged with putty, veined with cracks, stark white. The glass eyeballs are scoured milky by the seasons. A rag of bird's nest dangles in the wind from the antlers, the hide worn smooth in spots to the canvas beneath the nappy fur. The wind starts tears in my eyes, and I feel the spit of moisture in the wind against my cheeks.

Parker knew the only reason Tilly told him to hang around was because Parker had a pack of Luckies. Besides Parker and Tilly, the Booth brothers were there, and two other friends of Tilly's Parker had never seen before. Tilly pulled out the pint of Early Times when they were sitting out on the end of the dock to smoke.

Fearing What Dreams?

"You swipe that from your old man?" Parker asked. The Booth brothers laughed.

"Where'd the cat get his ass?" one of the other two said.

"Ask me no questions, I tell you no lies," Tilly said. They lit up Parker's cigarettes, and Tilly drank and passed the pint to each of his friends in turn. Parker didn't expect to get a swig.

"Your turn in the barrel," Tilly said. He wiped the neck of the bottle with the heel of his hand and held it out to Parker. Tilly's other friend called Parker a simp, and the Booth brothers laughed it up. "Suck up," Tilly said, "we'll get bombed and go get some poon."

Parker drank, passed the bottle, waited for his turn again. They chain-smoked his Lucky Strikes. To avoid looking at them, he looked back down the dock, past the beach to the brightly lit pavilion. The band played fast music. He could make out couples, pairs of girls jitterbugging. He didn't believe they would really go after girls when they finished Tilly's pint.

I am unable to eat the scrambled eggs, hash browns, and pork sausage I ordered. I drink my coffee black, for fear the milk in the jug on the counter may be soured. I smoke but do not lay the cigarette in the ashtray, crusted from rim to rim with cold ashes, emptied, but never washed or wiped clean. "Business," I say, "seems a little slow."

"Praise the Lord for small favors," says the waitress. She pushes grease toward a slot at the rear of the griddle with the edge of her spatula. She is nearly six feet tall, the thinnest woman I have ever seen. She wears no sanitary net over her hennaed hair. She is old. Purple veins stand in relief on the back of her liver-spotted hands. Her throat is slack, wrinkled as a turkey's. Her uniform dress is starched, clean, her white shoes unsmudged, but she wears no hose on her emaciated legs, and her short apron is filthy from leaning into the counter and the griddle's edge as she works. She wears a plastic name tag on her absolutely flat chest. Her name is Ollie.

She holds a cigarette in her mouth while she works. The ash grows long, then falls on the griddle when she moves her head. She does not notice the ash, turning to speak to the diseased man as much as to me. "I like to run my feet to stumps, Labor Day," Ollie says.

"Know just exactly what you mean," says the diseased man. I have seen pictures of tropical elephantiases victims. "I seen summer people enough to last me," he says. His voice booms, echoes, as if electronically amplified. Everything about him is swollen, inflated, enlarged. His mug of coffee is like a thimble in his puffy fingers. His voice rumbles out of a mouth wide as a mail slot, set above a jutting jaw so large it appears molded of clay or rubber, glued on. His black eyes are shadowed by bristly brows, like eaves. He wears denim coveralls, slouches at a table, too big for a counter stool, unlaced work shoes extended out into the aisle between tables and counter like packing boxes.

"Talk to me summer people," Ollie says. The diseased man laughs. I expect the window to rattle, the floor to shift under my stool. I smile to show I am listening, interested.

"Don't I know you?" says the only other customer. He sits two stools down from me. He has drunk three Alka-Seltzers since I arrived. His face is familiar. It is Harley Eagan, the real estate salesman and bromide addict. His skin is almost translucent under the fluorescent lighting.

"Parker. You may remember my parents if you don't remember me."

He does remember, already handing me his business card. "For sure," he says. "Parker. The big old place out on the lake road by Weller's there. I'm no good at faces much, but I never forget a property. I recall some effort to put you in touch with a buyer when that property came to you."

Fearing What Dreams?

"I wasn't selling," I say. He smokes his cigarettes in a short black and silver holder, licks his lips frequently, as if his mouth were perpetually dry. His teeth are so white and even they must be false. He is very natty, wears a dark grey straw hat with totemic feather in the band perched on the back of his head, a light grey Palm Beach suit, two-tone black-and-white shoes, a large diamond ring on his ring finger, a pearl tack in his tie, brushed silver digital wristwatch. He is very out of season, seen against the snow, like dust motes, dancing in the air outside when I check the window.

"Absetively posilutely," says Harley Eagan, swiveling on his stool to face me directly. "And would it be presumptuous to ask if you're up here now looking to unload that property?"

"No. I'm living out there now." It is as if Harley Eagan cannot hear me.

"Because this is the wrong time to sell," he says, waves to Ollie for another Alka-Seltzer.

"I'm living out there now."

"Spring," says Harley Eagan, "is the time to put lake frontage on the market. You look me up"—he points a finger at the business card I hold—"just before Memorial Day. I'll get you some top dollars or I'm not who I say I am." He turns to his fizzing glass. "Winter," says he, "we grind to a screeching halt hereabouts. All play and no work, Labor Day to Memorial Day, right, Ollie?" He winks hard at her, tips up his drink, gulps. I watch his throat move as he drinks it all, sets the glass on the counter, sighs.

"I'll give you play," Ollie says.

"I was born tired and ain't rested up enough since," says the diseased man. When he chuckles, it sounds like the throb of a motor.

"What are winters up here like?" I say, but they are talking to themselves.

Says Harley Eagan, "I only wish I could move lots off season like I do in spring. Goddamn me, I'm a buying and selling fool come spring!"

"If wishes was fishes I'd be a bird and fly me south to Florida, too," says Ollie, taking my money, making change.

"I wish I was a bear," says the diseased man. "I'd crawl inside a tree and sleep till I felt like getting up to eat." His voice resonates, more growl than speech.

Parker and his girl lay together in the hammock his grandfather had custom-made to hang between the two tallest Norway pines, just at the edge of the bluff. Parker could not remember it, but his mother told him he often shared it as a child with his napping grandfather on late, hot summer afternoons.

His girl lay in the crook of his arm as the hammock drifted. He felt no cramp in his arm, even though he had not moved in a long time. It was a hot day, but the whole of his girl's body felt cool alongside his in the hammock. It was the best place in all the world and time to be. He meant to say something better, but only said, "This is living," to his girl. She mumbled something, perhaps a word, a sigh, nothing he could understand, because she had dozed to a half-sleep there beside him.

"I'll get us a beer," he said, and went to the cottage. His mother was sweeping grits of sand from the kitchen linoleum. She had been weeping.

"What's the matter?" Parker said.

"Dirt," Parker's mother said, "fight it all your life, when you're dead they throw it in your face."

"Take a break," Parker said quickly, "we'll all three of us go into Wautoma and get a bite to eat or something."

"You go do what you like and leave other people alone, will you," his mother said to him.

Fearing What Dreams?

"I don't do almost no extra work no more," says Crazy John. "Why should I work extra if I don't need nothing? I got everything I need."

"I was hoping maybe I could persuade you," I say. "For old time's sake maybe. Maybe you remember my old man, Parker? You built a fireplace in our cottage for him, must be thirty years ago. One summer," I say, "you hauled the rock in from the quarry. I remember I helped you piss-ant rocks from your truck when you did it. That was me."

"I hardly never work special now," says Crazy John.

We stand just in front of the miniature chapel he built in memory of his mother. It is famous in the county, draws summer people with cameras in season, was featured in a tourism pamphlet produced by the state years ago. I would like to see inside, but he does not invite me. I would have to crouch to enter. It is dollhouse size, built of the native stone from which he built so many natural fireplaces and beach retaining walls out on Silver Lake.

"Winter's early," I say, lift my hand to the flakes suspended in the air about us. It is a light, soft snow, barely enough to veneer the grass, pleasant because the temperature is barely below freezing. It does not stick to the walls of Crazy John's memorial chapel.

Beyond the chapel is the small pond people call John's Lake. Off to the right is the shack he lives in, once a railroad freight car, dark smoke pouring out of the chimney pipe, spicing the air with the smell of burning oak and pine. "I need help to lay in a few cords of wood, winterize my cottage. You know all the secrets of it," I say.

"Ain't you summer people?"

"No. I was, for years. We came up summers from the time I was a baby, my father's father before him. I plan to live here, this winter at least. You knew my old man. Parker?" Snowflakes flick against my face, but it is not cold.

"I built with stone all my life, I can't recall all of it. Now I only work extra if I need something special." Crazy John wears an army surplus overcoat. He wears no hat. Snowflakes begin to stick in his hair and beard. His hair and beard and moustache grow together like an aura about his face, untrimmed, shot with streaks of white, brown-gold, red, like a sunburst framing his face. His lips are stained, as if he chewed tobacco or sucked snuff, but I do not see him spit or swallow noticeably. His shoes are cracked and greasy, laces broken and reknotted. If we were in his shack with the stove roaring, I know he would stink terribly.

"See, John, I need some help. I need to hole up out there a while. I have some thinking to do, I think." It feels a little colder, the flakes smaller, but more of them, blowing in the air. The ground is almost all white now.

"I think all the time," says Crazy John. "Even when I'm working special to get something special I need, I'm all the time thinking." He pats the head of the mixed breed setter that plays about his legs, whining softly, as if it has begun to feel the cold now. At the door of his shack, a cat sits, tail curled over its front paws, waiting for him to take them all inside to the warmth. Except when petting his dog, Crazy John's hands are motionless at his sides. His hands are grimy, knuckles barked, nails dirty. They do not look like particularly strong hands, able to build so wonderfully with stone.

"John, please help me get my cottage ready for winter," I say. The snow thickens. I feel the cold. It is hard to see the whole of the pond called John's Lake through the swirling snow. Some of the snow sticks to the stone roof and walls of his chapel. His dog yelps, prances about us.

"I don't know for sure," he says. "Maybe I'll come out tomorrow if I can think of something I need to work extra for. The lake road by Weller's?"

"Parker," I say, "you can't miss it." I step past him, peer in the window no larger than a sheet of paper, cup my hands to examine the reduced perfection of the altar, organ, pews with hymnals in the racks, like a doll's-house church waiting for a congregation of children to come worship. I wonder, if there were a service, would it be Crazy John who preached, or is the tiny pulpit open to anyone feeling the call of the spirit?

Her father sat Parker and his fiancée down for an old-fashioned talk after they told him they were going to get married.

"We're not talking fun and games, are we," he said. "We're talking a lifetime for two people. Do you have any idea what it takes to build a life? Not play house, build something lasts forever until death do us part."

"Are you asking me if I know what life is all about or something? I'm not sure what you're asking me," Parker said.

"You just give me a listen here," his future father-in-law said, and went on to give Parker and his daughter a long and serious talking to about life, how hard it was, the problems, probably pitfalls. Parker and his fiancée held hands. His fiancée smiled at her father as he talked. Parker nodded his head from time to time, smiled when her father was smiling, showing him he was serious and interested.

Later, he and his father-in-law considered the lecture a family joke, laughed whenever anyone alluded to it. But Parker saw no humor in it. He had no opinion about it. The plain truth was he remembered little of it. He had not really been listening.

"Such justice as there is, you're looking at it," says Sheriff Lou Dutcher. "Summers I got three deputies and a jailer besides the township constable, what with summer people and all."

"I used to see him," I say, "old guy directing traffic at the intersection by the old post office during the season."

"You're thinking of old Schaeffer," the sheriff says, "up and died on me a few years back. We got a young fellow was in the military police in Vietnam works the township summers now."

"I haven't been up the last several years," I say.

"What I can't understand is your coming up this time of year at all," he says.

"I'm not sure I understand it myself. I just thought you'd appreciate knowing in advance it wasn't a hobo broke in my cottage to get warm if you happen to see lights out there some night."

He has a fine jail and courthouse, stone construction, a WPA project, as solid as if Crazy John had built it by hand. A block off Wautoma's main street, it sits back on a broad lawn decorated by a Civil War statue, cannon, stacked cannonballs, a roll of honor for the war dead of a hundred years.

"Summer," says Sheriff Dutcher, "you'd be lucky to catch me casual like this. I'm always out. If it's not two migrant workers cutting each other's faces off with knives or broken bottles, it's some city kid drowning himself in Silver Lake or some laker setting the woods on fire to burn his trash in a high wind."

"Laker?"

"Summer people," says the sheriff. "There's people don't have the brains God give geese."

His office is large and very neat. Federal wanted posters are tacked in rows on a cork bulletin board. Three shotguns are padlocked in a varnished rack. He wears no uniform, could pass for a retired man employed as caretaker, a plainly but neatly dressed trusty. A large radio sits on his desk, dials lighted, but there is no sound from it. We can hear the wind blowing the snow hard outside the barred window. There is a good smell of cooking in the room, from the jail kitchen down the corridor. Mrs. Dutcher is there, preparing dinner for the sheriff. When he has prisoners, she is paid for cooking their meals and cleaning cells. "I'm budgeted one deputy off-season," he says, "so I keep it in the family."

"I'm keeping you from eating," I say. "I just wanted to let you know I'm out there now. I don't imagine I'll need to call on you for protection." I try to laugh. "If this was Chicago it'd be something else again. They'll raid your house with you in it if they get the notion."

"I never try to predict," Sheriff Lou Dutcher says. He is not joking. Only a few years ago he made the news in Chicago, nationwide. It was the dead of winter when the Wild Rose murderer was discovered. Hollywood made a movie about it, and the book became a best-seller.

"Imagine me," says the sheriff, "smack in the middle of deer season, kid from Wild Rose finds a human head stuck up in a tree, hair still on it, but you couldn't tell the sex of it for the shape it was in by that time."

"I never did get to see the movie, but I saw the news reports." The sheriff shakes his head.

"Old coot gone stark staring mad living out to his mother's farm he inherited, you know. People didn't even know she was dead. Kept her right in the house there with him. God and the devil knows what got him carving up old ladies. They went and made their movie of it out in California. We were still finding bones and parts up to two years ago. That's one time you didn't catch me casual in the office."

"I can imagine." Mrs. Dutcher closes a door loudly down the corridor. Her husband checks his watch, turns a dial on the desk radio until we hear static.

"See if Tilly's yakking with all his gals on the citizen's band," he says.

"I know Tilly. Summers, when I was a kid," I say.

The sheriff says, "Sometimes the Mrs. and me sit here when the TV reception's poor, eavesdrop him calling all over the county with those gals. I always figure, anything really bad happens out there in the boonies, Tilly'll call me on channel nine."

"Your dinner will be getting cold," I say.

"I hope you got a four-wheel vehicle for when the snow really flies here."

I say, "This won't last." It is too dark now to see the snow-filled air through the barred window.

"Says my Aunt Fanny," says the sheriff. "I've seen it blow up drifts three feet high in early September. I've seen it snow in October so food ran out in the restaurant. Mr. Parker," he says, "one spring back it was we found a fellow got lost hunting deer the year before, took me and then some to be sure it wasn't another of our Wild Rose ones, which they proved it was wolves or some animals carried away parts of this one. Scientifically," he says. "The only thing I count on is not counting on anything."

If his wife had been there, Parker knew he would not have talked that way. "I get it exactly," Parker said, "I get it with the purple shaft with barbs on, right where the sun don't shine."

"Mr. Parker," his wife's lawyer said.

"Oh holy balls!" Parker said. "What it comes down to is I can keep enough to buy a barrel if I agree to live in the barrel and eat the rain, right?"

"Mr. Parker, can I remind you that no matter what there's a future to be faced, and we all have to live in it?" her lawyer said.

"What future?" Parker said. "Chew me dry, spit me out, that's a future? Where the hell you come from, Jack?"

The lawyer said, "We can meet another time."

"We can meet in hell's half-acre," Parker said. "Screw it," he said, "go on, sock it to me. What the hell do I care? My old man

always told me there's no pockets in shrouds. I can see you enjoy this. Tell me, can you sleep nights? Do you enjoy more widows and orphans, or am I your favorite? Go ahead write it up, I'll sign it. Try not to drool on the paper."

He said more of that kind of thing, and the lawyer sat through it, and they finished up their business. Nothing he said provoked the lawyer.

Tilly looks a lot older than I do. "Tilly," I say, "I wouldn't have known you without the sign outside to tell me."

"Sure, Parker," says Tilly, "and you're exactly the same as you were twenty-five years ago, I suppose?" He is not joking; we do not laugh. He moves down the bar to serve a drink. He is a good bartender, always serves a napkin with a drink, keeps the ashtrays on the bar emptied. I check myself in the backbar mirror. The mirror is tinted blue. I look younger than Tilly does, though we are the same age.

Tilly has let himself go over the years. When we were boys, what impressed me most about him was his adult indifference. His paunch and spare tire roll over his wide, white leather belt. His formfitting white denims are much too tight. His shape is roughly that of a squat pear. The early cold front with snow has caught him still dressed for Indian summer, a short-sleeve pullover and canvas deck shoes. The pullover is too tight. Tilly looks hermaphroditic, amply breasted, six-month pregnancy. The wiry mat of hair at his throat and on his forearms has grizzled. He is balding, only a monk's tonsure remaining, a few long strands combed across his scalp and his smooth, swarthy forehead.

I say, "You know, somehow I always knew you weren't the marrying kind, Tilly. You'd like Chicago, it's full of singles bars, swinger clubs, you name it." In the blue-tinted mirror, the grey hair emerging at my temples and above my ears is not visible.

"Parker," says Tilly, "didn't you never hear you don't buy the cow when the milk's free?" We smile as if we thought it truly funny.

"Break one-niner for the Big T. Stinger," comes loudly over Tilly's CB base radio. He boasts his roof antenna can pull in Mt. Morris and Wild Rose, as far as Oshkosh on a day with proper atmospherics. This snowfall has shortened his range. Tilly grins at me as he picks up his microphone to answer.

"You got the Stingeroo," he says, leers, raises his eyebrows. "Blondie?" he says. "Now hear this," Tilly says to me as he waits for her response. The other customers in the bar, locals, stop talking, listen along with Tilly whenever the CB is active.

"Very funny, Tilly," says the radio.

"Ain't supposed to use real names on CB, sweets," says Tilly. "Give us a report on all this fluff stuff coming down outside. Use your right handle now." The locals wait for Tilly's leer, until he has released the microphone button, before they laugh, softly, so as not to obscure a quick call back from her. But she does not speak again. Tilly sneers. "That's the Wildflower," he says to me. "All uptight when I play like I think it's somebody else."

"Who's Blondie?" I ask. Tilly whistles, rolls his eyes toward the ceiling, brings his fingertips together in front of his chest in mock prayer.

"I guess it's good to have a hobby to keep you from going stir-crazy over the winter," I say. He shrugs. I notice he does not drink much. When someone buys a round for the house, he takes a cigar rather than a drink. I cannot decide if I loathe or admire his lack of concern.

"Break one-nine" he says into his microphone. "Big T. Stinger for Wildflower. You got your ears on, hon? Come on, Wildflower," he is saying. "Give us your twenty. Don't you love me no more, Wildflower?"

I say, "You're smart, Tilly. A good bar's a gold mine. One of my main mistakes was getting in with my ex's old man. Grain futures. Fat one quarter, famine the next. Maybe what I should have done was buy myself a business like yours. How much does a base rig like that cost?"

"This is Blondie. Come back," says the CB radio.

"Like hell it is," Tilly says, turns to face his customers, who hush to follow this. "Come in see us, Wildflower," he says, "I'll mix you a tall one up'll curl your toes, sweet."

"What I'm curious to see now," I say, "is how I take to solitude. Some people can't be alone too much. There's a thin edge you can't let yourself cross."

"Got your ears on, Stinger?" Wildflower says, giggles. I have to talk louder to be heard.

"See, Tilly, my trouble is I don't have any roots any more. I'm beginning to wonder if I ever did. What I want to do is figure out something to do for the rest of my life. Such as it is," I say.

Tilly says, "Still waiting on your twenty, Wildflower. You better get in here, that fluff's coming down hard, babes. Talk to me, sweet."

"Tilly," I say, "did you ever stop at any one point in your life and try to think about the past, and find you couldn't remember a thing? Way back, when we were kids, summers, did you plan your life? What's bothering me is, if you don't have a past you can understand, how in hell can I have a future? Can you tell me how we get when and where we are, Tilly?"

"You can go piss up a rope!" says his CB radio. Tilly looks to his customers to laugh it up for him.

"Tilly, can you give me just one minute to listen to me for a minute?" I rub a spot clear in the frost on his window. The snow is falling, blowing.

"Hey, Parker," he says as I leave, "they teach you how to drive in this stuff without sliding upside down in the ditch down in Chicago?"

The evening of the last day Parker spent with his family, in his Skokie home, he helped put his sons to bed, then asked his wife if she would sit up a while with him and talk. They sat in the den, but even after the boys were sound asleep in their rooms, they did not talk, just sat there as far apart as they could sit in the den.

Finally his wife got up and said this was ridiculous, she was going to bed. He asked if she cared if he sat there a while longer before he left. She said she did not care what he did. She went to bed and he sat there a long time before he got up to leave.

Before he left he went to the open doors to his sons' bedrooms. He could see them very clearly, sleeping soundly, in the moonlight from their windows and the light from the hall. The two doors were side by side, so he could stand in the hall and see them both sleeping, hear their regular breathing.

They slept so deeply, their breathing so relaxed and even. It was so clear to him that they were untroubled, by their own lives, by what was happening to their parents, untroubled by any dreams as they slept. Parker left the house quietly, careful to catch the lock on the front door as he left, not disturb his wife or sleeping children.

The image of their sleeping, his sensation of the quality of their sleep, stayed with Parker for a long time. He thought nothing particular about it, came to no conclusions. It was what he noticed, what impressed him most, what came back to his mind when he happened to think that he had left his family and home forever.

I will sleep with my clothes on. Dressed, under the damp old quilt smelling of long storage, face pressed into the musty pillow, heating it with my breath, I try to warm myself enough to get to sleep.

It is possible a man could die here. I think it is possible, but I do not think it is likely, probable. I do not dwell on it. I do not wish to think of anything but cannot help thinking how very cold I feel, that I could die here this night if I am not able to warm myself.

I could get up, make my way through the snowdrifts on foot to Weller's tavern. Even in this total dark, writhing with snow, I think I could walk that far, find the lake road, the highway, the mounted moose's head caked with snow, bang on his door, yell louder than the wind to wake him. That would be risky. Wally may be passed out, lost in his stupor to my voice, the storm, asleep without even knowing he is asleep, that he is warm and sleeping through the first blizzard of winter.

I try to warm myself. I remember that I can hope old Crazy John will start his truck, puts chains on the tires, cut through to my cottage tomorrow, plow out my drive, bring me wood for the fireplace. I imagine his memorial chapel, white with snow, door sealed by drifts, Crazy John's converted railroad freight car a block of white snow in the black night, John and his dog and cat snug inside, cozy, needing nothing, smoke rising from his stovepipe into the sky, blending with the billows of snow in the air. I know Crazy John will not come through the blocked roads to me tomorrow. I cannot make myself warm. I begin to think I will die here this night.

I am not sure how afraid I am, think it may be only that I am so cold. The cold is a deep, hard pain I feel. I try to see if I am really afraid to die.

I imagine I have frozen to death in the night. I imagine it is day, the storm over, the sun out bright and clear as it was on Labor Day. The woods and roads are covered with a drifted, rolling coat of very white snow. Silver Lake is calm, the water very black looking against the white shores. It is still quite cold, but the sun shines. The snow cover glitters as if it held millions of specks of glass or mica. It is so bright and white it hurts my eyes to look at all the snow reflecting the hard sunlight.

I imagine I have frozen to death in my clothes, under the crazy-quilt. Someone must find me, know I am dead if I am to imagine what it is like to be dead, to see if I am really afraid to die. I imagine how this happens.

Harley Eagan sits in the diner, drinking Alka-Seltzer, contemplating the big bucks he will earn when the spring brings lake frontage back on the market. The diseased man broods about being a bear in hibernation, dwarfing his chair. Ollie scrapes grease from the griddle, wiggles the toes of her sore feet inside her white shoes for relief. Sheriff Lou Dutcher enters, making a routine round after the storm. They talk. I am mentioned in passing. The diseased man says summer people have no business in the county after Labor Day. Ollie says her feet hurt too much to talk about anything. Harley Eagan gives the sheriff precise directions to my property.

That afternoon, or the next, or the next, sometime during the iron grip of this winter, he comes and finds me here. I am frozen to death, wrapped like a mummy in my clothes, the quilt, face hidden in the pillow. I am frozen to death, like a lump of earth and rags, as cold within as without, as the snow or the air.

Sheriff Dutcher radios a report to his wife at the courthouse and jail. He is overheard on the police band by Tilly, who idly monitors his receiver as he waits for customers to come drink away the frozen day.

I am not afraid to die. I am so cold, it is natural to wish to be warm, but I do not fear dying. I think of nothing. I do not wish to think of anything. There is no other place I would rather be. I am simply very tired. I would like to sleep. I try not to hear the storm howl outside the cottage. I will try to sleep. I do not fear any dreams I may have.

THE AMERICAN DREAM
The Book of Boggs

In the Oklahoma Panhandle, in the vicinity of the Texas border, lived a man named T. Boone Boggs. And this T. Boone Boggs did prosper mightily, and was wondrously content, and was full of praise and good works for the Lord. And he did bask in the benevolence of the Lord, who watched over him and did guard him against the misfortunes that may befall a man in life.

This T. Boone Boggs, upon arising each morning, did turn to his wife and say, "Praise the Lord, Jeanmarie, ain't this the life though!" And his wife was wont always to reply that it did appear that they had been blessed. And after arising from their king-size round bed, and after performing their daily ablutions in the gleaming double bathroom of the master bedroom, T. Boone Boggs and his wife did, each morning, walk through the patio doors that gave entrance to a redwood deck, where-from they might look upon the landscape and know the plea-sure of all that had come to them in life. And T. Boone Boggs with his wife did look out upon the world and consider what he saw as his reward for his unstinting labor and the righteousness of his ways in the service of the Lord. "Hoo boy!" he was wont to say to his wife, "Jeanmarie, did you ever once think we'd be riding this high on the hog? Praise the Lord, hon, and thanks to a little help from old Cletus Dalrymple, wherever he is, and the oil depletion laws, and my having such good sense for business!"

"I'll confess I never thought you'd become a corporate tycoon, Boone," his wife, Jeanmarie, was wont to say to him.

Close at hand, they did look upon the ornamental shrubs and the banks of bright flowers blooming in beds cultivated by their full-time Mexican gardener, Patricio Sandoval, who was already at work, his bare, muscled back gleaming with sweat in the bright sun of morning. And they did look upon the crushed gravel drive that formed a great white arc before the massive Spanish doors of their half-million-dollar split-level home, paid for in cash less than a year before. And they looked upon the broad expanse of their barbered lawn, the rich green of carpet grass dotted here and there with the shapes of live oak, magnolia, cedar, and pine, in the branches of which mockingbirds and cardinals and jays sang in praise of the new day.

And T. Boone Boggs did lift his eyes to look upon the boundaries of his property, marked with a white rail fence, and did lift his eyes yet higher to look into the distance. There he did discern the black shafts of oil rigs alternating with pumpers and storage tanks, and beyond them the misty bulk of Boggs Refinery, Inc., looming like a small mountain on the flatness of the Panhandle, and farther did he look, to the small town of Goshen, Oklahoma, where above the roofs of the homes of his refinery workers shone the tower of the Crystal Palace of God's People, a bright needle thrust upward through the drifting refinery haze, a great church built by T. Boone Boggs as witness to his love of the Lord.

"Jeanmarie," he did say to his wife, "do you ever think sometimes how mysterious it is we are so blessed? I mean, where did old Cletus Dalrymple run off to just when I struck it rich? What must he be thinking now if he reads about me in *Time* or *U.S. News & World Report* or *Business Week*, or about me building the Crystal Palace and getting Reverend Dr. Vardis Klemp to be its preacher if he reads in *Christianity Today* or one of them others wrote me up? Oh, Jeanmarie, praise to the Lord and hard work is what it is!" he did say to his wife.

And his wife did say, "Boone, did you ever look at that Mexican Patricio when he's working with his shirt off? Lordy, how them muscles is all shiny rippling in his back from sweating!"

And as he broke his fast each morning with fried eggs and whole-hog sausage and Texas toast and strong, black coffee in the breakfast nook of his half-million-dollar house, sitting across from his wife and his daughter, Mary Helen, the heart of T. Boone Boggs was overfilled with the rapture of his knowledge of all that had come to him and was his in this life.

And he did consider the facts of his life. He did consider that, though his own mama and daddy were only poor country people from Payne County, Oklahoma, now dead and gone, they had been hardworking, God-fearing folk who suffered and survived the Dust Bowl on a hardscrabble farm, and had raised him in righteousness and the discipline of hard labor by which to earn his bread. And he did consider his still-lovely wife, Jeanmarie, who had placed third runner-up in the Miss Oklahoma pageant of 1961. And he did consider his beautiful little daughter, Mary Helen, who sat across from him in her cheerleader's uniform, and who was active in 4-H and Junior Achievement. And T. Boone Boggs thought of his son, T. Boone, Jr., away at the University of Oklahoma to study petroleum engineering, and the heart of T. Boone Boggs was gorged on pride and love for the wonderful family that had come to him in life.

And there was yet more for the thoughts of T. Boone Boggs to dwell upon as he rose from the breakfast nook to begin his day's work. He thought of all he possessed, of his half-million-dollar home with extensive grounds tended by the full-time Mexican gardener, Patricio Sandoval, and of the huge garage in which were parked his vehicles, a matched pair of Cadillacs and a Datsun 280-Z and a gentleman's pickup he drove in memory of his humble beginnings. He thought of his Olympic-size pool and his sauna and of the tennis courts and of the stable where his daughter's horses neighed for their oats. He thought of the walk-in closets that held his wardrobe, and of the closets of his wife and daughter and his absent son. And the thoughts of T. Boone Boggs whirled to a blur of all that he owned that he might reach out and touch at any moment he wished.

And there was yet more. In the bank of Goshen, Oklahoma, in a vault, were stock certificates and promissory notes and government bonds and letters of credit and certificates of option on mineral rights to likely acreage all over America's Southwest, and deeds to land and rent-houses and apartment buildings and nursing homes and motels and supermarkets. And all these were his and were managed for him by hosts of shrewd lawyers and accountants. And there was even a leather sack of Krugerrands, purchased more on a whim than as a hedge against unbridled inflation. And there was, of course, much cash in various accounts.

All this he knew, and took great joy of it, and praised the Lord for it, and knew that it was the product of great labor on his part, and perhaps a bit of luck, and did momentarily wonder what had become of Cletus Dalrymple, with whom it all began years ago. And he said to his wife and daughter, "I got to get in to work. The Lord gives us a day and then it's up to us to make the most of it."

And his daughter bade him good day, and so did his wife, and she said further to him, "I got to find that Mexican Patricio and tell him not to work around the house with his body half-naked. It don't look right with Mary Helen seeing him half-naked."

And T. Boone Boggs did set forth in his gentleman's pickup

truck in the direction of Goshen, where lay his refinery and his corporate headquarters and the Crystal Palace of God's People, Reverend Dr. Vardis Klemp, Pastor, which church had been built by Boggs to praise the Lord for his benevolence.

And the Lord looked down upon His man T. Boone Boggs there in the Oklahoma Panhandle and was well pleased with him. And He did say to Satan, "Can I pick 'em or can I pick 'em, Nick? You got to grant Me old Boggs there is going some!"

And Satan said, "Big deal."

"Sour grapes," said the Lord.

And Satan said unto the Lord, "Sure your boy Boggs does right. And why shouldn't he, what with all You done for him? Didn't You marry him to a ex-beauty queen and give him two picture-book kids? And didn't You send him that angel in the form of a independent oilfield speculator named Cletus Dalrymple who convinced him to drop out of the A&M college of Stillwater and go wildcatting wells out to the Panhandle? Which angel Cletus Dalrymple then put him onto mineral leases at rock-bottom prices and set his rigs up over the biggest pockets of black gold since Teapot Dome and Anadarko Basin, big as Spindletop practically! And then when he was pumping gushers, then what'd You go and do for him?" Satan did ask of the Lord.

"Okay, so I give him a nudge up to start," the Lord said.

"Nudge!" Satan did cry out. "I'd say *nudge*! You went and had them Arabs embargo oil is what You done! You created your Boggs a energy crisis is what You done! You decontrolled wellhead prices is all You done for him! You made him a energy tycoon almost overnight is what-all You done!"

"Calm down, Nick," said the Lord. "Okay, so I helped him. But he was a good boy to start with. His old mama and daddy was good country folks from up near to Stillwater, went through My Dust Bowl with nary a whimper, and they raised little

T. Boone up righteous. You don't see My system. Folks do good works because they believe in the possible rewards of it. I just give T. Boone some of the fruits coming to him and his folks both."

"Fruits?" said Satan unto the Lord. "I'd call them *fruits* and them some. No wonder he funds half the charities in his part of the Panhandle, giving generously for senior centers and day-care for his refinery people, donated dialysis machines to a mess of hospitals I recollect, sponsors Junior Achievement and 4-H and recreational fast-pitch softball and Good Government Day in Tulsa and Oklahoma City both, oh, he is a pure-fire monument to faith and works, he is, witnessing at all them Chamber of Commerce prayer breakfasts too, don't he!"

And the Lord said, "Your trouble is you don't like giving credit for credit due, Nick. You-all are forgetting that chair he endowed at the University of Oklahoma, and the big pledge he just made for a Free Enterprise Center on the Norman campus, and also how about all those under-the-table athletic scholar-ships? Which is not even to speak of the Crystal Palace of God's People there in Goshen. And how are you liking the success of Reverend Dr. Vardis Klemp now he's getting media attention with his book, *Corporate Capitalism: God's Way*? First one he ever wrote, and it's a big hit! 'Fess up, Nick, you are just plain contrary."

And Satan said, "What I say is, take some of them fruits away from him, see how righteous he stays. You and your system. It only works when You make it do!"

"Are you daring Me, Nick?" asked the Lord.

"I double dare You," Satan said.

"That ties it!" said the Lord, and He was exceeding wroth, and Satan did tremble for fear of the Lord's anger. And then the Lord was calmed, and said unto Satan, "Okay. You go have a crack at T. Boone Boggs there and we'll just see."

"Carte blanche?" asked Satan.

"To a point," answered the Lord. "You can hit him in his bankbook, and you can grieve him through his family, and I don't give a rap for his reputation in Oklahoma or Texas neither one, and you can trouble him some personally, but I don't want to hear about him being no way damaged permanent physically."

"Got you," Satan did say. "I know the ways of it. I will maybe show up Your system for something folks will sour on when they see it go bad on them of a sudden."

"Your trouble, Nick," said the Lord unto Satan, "is you never think big enough. My system works out of its bigness."

"Just watch me do!" said Satan.

"I plan to," said the Lord.

And the decline of the fortunes of T. Boone Boggs was rapid and complete. The Arab oil embargo was lifted, and American industry, its markets shrinking in a worldwide recession, its ability to borrow venture capital inhibited by high interest rates, did sharply reduce the national demand for energy fuels, and the American motoring public did practice fuel conservation. And it came to pass that there was an international oil glut. And so it was that the corporate finances of T. Boone Boggs were found to be vastly overextended, and the consortium of lenders who had assured his line of credit were loath to continue their support of his endeavors, and did, instead, call upon him and all his agents to meet their debts, refusing, at the last, to refinance both his long- and short-term notes, and bankers in Oklahoma and Texas and Illinois and Pennsylvania were ruined in the debacle. And even, wondrously, such few new holes as T. Boone Boggs did manage to drill were all found to be dusters.

And there came soon the day of reckoning, when all was lost, and his corporation and all its subsidiary companies were declared bankrupt, and what little remained of his life's work was placed in the hands of a federal receivership, and the nation's politicians were called upon to speak soothing words to cushion the shock to the stock market. And the news of this disaster was reported for all to read in the pages of *Time* and *U.S. News & World Report* and *Business Week.*

And T. Boone Boggs did say to his wife, Jeanmarie, "I don't understand the first part of it! Ever'thing was going so right, and now look at the pickle I'm in!"

And his wife did say to him, "You got too big for your britches is what you done. Now it's come to me keeping house in a rented trailer like it was twenty years ago, I suppose? Not this gal, Boone!"

And he lost not only his corporate holdings, but also his personal fortune, to include even his sack of Krugerrands, and his half-million-dollar home was taken for sale at public auction, and he and his wife and his daughter went to live in a trailer court on the outskirts of Goshen, Oklahoma, and the name of T. Boone Boggs had become anathema in the land.

And even more did he lose. His daughter, Mary Helen, was made pregnant out of wedlock by the feckless son of an oilfield roustabout, and she did flee to live in sin with the boy in Odessa, Texas. And though he did grieve for shame, his wife was no comfort to him in his misery, saying, "Maybe you should of give her a taste of your belt once in a while instead of being so busy being a tycoon, she might of turned out better."

Nor did he find comfort in his son and namesake, for T. Boone, Jr., was dismissed from the University of Oklahoma for selling cannabis and amphetamine tablets on the Norman campus, and his son did flee to a religious commune in Colorado, and did change his name to New Child of Chemical Light, and did refuse all communication with his parents.

And T. Boone Boggs was utterly disconsolate, and did sit,

drinking a bottle of Pearl beer, in the rented trailer that was now his home and his exile. And he did cry out to his wife, "It ain't any justice to it! That boy has disgraced us! Now they ain't even going to name that endowed chair after me there!" And his wife was no comfort, saying their son's depravity was no worse than his father's failure, and further, what did he think Cletus Dalrymple thought of him now if he read the newspapers or watched television? And T. Boone Boggs did cry in his beer, and said, "If it wasn't for you and the hope I get reading Preacher Vardis Klemp's book, I don't believe I could go on!"

And then his wife, Jeanmarie, did tell him she was leaving him to live with another man, their former gardener, Patricio Sandoval, for life with T. Boone Boggs was too depressing. "It ain't no way fair!" he did cry out.

"We're shooting for a new life, me and Patricio. We're going to California where's he's got relatives own a greenhouse and landscaping business will give us a start. No hard feelings, Boone, but I just believe you are snake-bit."

And so great was the despair of T. Boone Boggs that he knew not where to turn for succor save the Reverend Dr. Vardis Klemp, Pastor of the Crystal Palace of God's People. And he did go to a pay telephone and called this divine, and did speak with the Reverend Dr.'s executive secretary, who did inform him that the Reverend was unavailable, being out on the road on an extended tour of bookstores and radio and television interviews to promote his new book, *Grace: God's Tax Shelter*.

"Lady," he did say to the executive secretary, "this is T. Boone Boggs speaking. I'm the man kicked in the lion's share to erect that glass church of yours. I'm hurting. My businesses is all bust, my wife's run off to California with a Mexican, my son's a hippie doper in Colorado last I heard of him, and my little girl's knocked up by a no-account and living in Odessa, Texas, on the Welfare for all I know. And if that ain't enough,

I'm suffering attacks of ulcers and hemorrhoids, and my hair's took to falling out in clumps all of a sudden!"

"I'm sorry, Mr. Boggs," she did say to him, "but the Reverend's out of touch. Maybe you could catch him on Carson tomorrow night? He talks as much about spiritual things as he does his new book on them shows."

And T. Boone Boggs, in the throes of despairing rage, did shout over the phone, "Then damn you all and damn it all if I ever give a pure damn for anything ever again and damn me for ever taking the advice of that damn Cletus Dalrymple!"

And Satan did say to the Lord, "How You like them apples?"

And the Lord said, "You pushed him pretty hard, Nick."

"You give me leave to," Satan said.

"It's a disappointment," the Lord did say, "but he was speaking in pain and the heat of the moment there. I might could still salvage something good out of him yet."

And Satan did say, "Oh, don't I know it! I suppose now You'll drop some new windfall on him. I can just see it, You'll send him another angel, maybe in the form of a electronics expert with a patent on a new generation mini-computer, make him rich all over again, won't You!"

"That'll do," the Lord said, and Satan was silent, and waited upon the Lord. And then He did say to Satan, "Nick, your trouble is you take the short view every time. Send down angels? Quick-fix him? Not likely! What it is is it takes the long haul to know a man's worth or bring it out either one."

"So what do You calculate doing?" Satan asked the Lord.

"Just you watch Me and see," said the Lord.

And T. Boone Boggs did sleep but fitfully in his rented trailer on the outskirts of Goshen, Oklahoma, crying out, *Why me? Why me!* and *Cletus Dalrymple, where are you when I need you!*

The American Dream: The Book of Boggs

And the Lord spoke to T. Boone Boggs in a dream, saying:

It ain't for you to question, Boggs. I'll say what's to be. Now hush up and hear Me. First off, you're well shut of that Jeanmarie. Second, your son's confused now, but I aim to send him a revelation soon. Before you know it, he'll be living clean and witnessing for Me, and I may just make him a media evangelist, seeing how tacky that Vardis Klemp turned out. And your little Mary Helen's going to get religion too. She'll birth a fine son and name him for you, and that boy'll comfort your old age.

As for you, you just ain't cut out for corporate success nor celebrity neither one. Maybe I should of left you to work your daddy's homestead over to Stillwater all your days. Messed up like you are, it's hurt the whole idea of rewards for faith and works. So what I reckon for you now is just that: faith and work! You'll have a good restful sleep now, and you'll wake up with that faith back strong forever. And then you'll set to work again because you got it back. You'll sweat like a Mexican all your days with a will because you'll believe the rewards are coming your way for it. Oh, you'll make wages, but that's all. The good of it is the example you'll set all those folks got disillusioned when your businesses collapsed so sudden and your reputation turned all sour. This way, folks making wages like you do will get believing again because they see you sweating and still believing. It will keep My system going.

Now stop your fussing, Boggs, and sleep on it. This is how it'll be, and there's an end on it!

And T. Boone Boggs woke refreshed and filled with a great faith in the day and all days to come. And he did live out his days in peace, laboring at such menial tasks as came his way, to include pumping gasoline, cooking short orders, and hiring out in the annual wheat harvests in the Oklahoma Panhandle. And his example was a powerful witness to all about him who dreamed the American Dream of rewards for faith and works. For they said: if T. Boone Boggs, who got rich in the oil business practically overnight and then went broke even faster, can sweat for a dollar and never miss church meetings Sundays or Wednesday evenings either one, who are we to say the system can't work for us?

And the life of T. Boone Boggs was counted a great success, and his old age was comforted by the presence of his only grandson, T. Boone III, and by his joy at the success of his son, T. Boone, Jr., who became regionally famous for his radio preaching.

"The odds, I grant you," T. Boone Boggs did say to those who came to hear him, "are heavy against it happening twice, but I can tell you I made it fast and fat once, and I do believe in my heart if I stay at the wheel I might could make it again, Lord willing!"

And Satan did say to the Lord, "You got a funny notion of justice."

And the Lord was not moved and said unto Satan, "It ain't nothing about justice in it, Nick. What it is is it works for most people as long as they think it does. The main thing is to keep it going, which is what it is with any system. Just look at old Boggs grunting away at it down there if you don't believe Me. And there's an end on it!"

And the Lord looked down upon T. Boone Boggs there in the Panhandle of Oklahoma and was well pleased with His man.

POET-IN-RESIDENCE

❧

> *Poets are the unacknowledged*
> *legislators of the world.*
> —*Percy Bysshe Shelley*

I am not a contentious man, do not like to argue, but they call themselves poets! I know better!

We meet: at college poetry readings, at workshops, at city-wide festivals, at autograph parties in bookstores and shopping malls—I have a professional obligation, after all, to keep up with the field—and they introduce themselves to me as *poets;* I try not to smirk, try to conceal my amusement and contempt, say nothing that might give away what I know, what I feel when they come up to me and tell me they are poets.

I am polite. I shake hands, and if it is true, I tell them I have read their poems—this delights them!—and I tell them I am a poet too. They make no effort to conceal their surprise, and when I tell them about my poetry, what sort of poet I am, they are not shy about expressing *their* disbelief, *their* amusement, *their* contempt, *their* self-righteous, self-serving sense of infinite superiority.

None of them has ever read any of my poems, and they do not ask to read them. I betray no hurt at this. I smile, congratulate them on their poetry, wish them all possible success with their work in the future. It is enough for me that I know I am a poet, and that they only pretend—what I mean to say is, they *pose* as poets; I do not. I know what a poet is, and I am a poet, which is really all there is to it!

"Hi," says Prinslow, who pretends to be a poet, when I approach him after his public reading at the Fine Arts Center. Says he: "I kept trying to make eye contact with you while I was up there at the lectern, but you were staring at the ceiling."

"I'm Darcy," I tell him, "I like to shut out everything except the words so I can concentrate."

"I was afraid maybe my stuff was turning you off," he says.

"Not at all. On the contrary. I especially like your anti-sonnets. I read that sequence you read from when it was published in the double anniversary issue of *Poetry*. I'm a poet too," I tell this Prinslow, the current favorite of little-magazine reviewers; he has received two National Endowment fellowships and a Guggenheim for his work, says he will go to live in Rome for a year to edit the volume of new and selected poems a New York publisher is impatient to print.

"Darcy?" says he.

"Darcy," I say. "I'm Poet-In-Residence at Acme. I doubt you've seen any of my work; I don't publish in literary magazines."

"Acme? You mean the company?"

"Acme, yes. Acme is a multinational corporation. It began as Communications Matrix, Inc., but we changed the name to Acme when we made the big move to diversification—electronics, satellites, mainframe computers, remote-sensing, laser focus guidance systems—we're big," I tell this Prinslow, who calls himself a poet.

Says he (laughing): "You're putting me on."

"No," I say, and show him my laminated, electric beam–sensitive identification card. "The red stripe," I explain, "means I can enter any office, any production facility, any laboratory I choose. I have access to any file. I know all the computer codes. I can attend any meeting I want. It's part of my job as Poet-In-Residence."

"Hey," he says, and his laugh is uncertain. "Pulling my leg, right? What the hell's a corporation got to do with poetry, right? Come off it, man!"

"I was never more serious," I say.

"Darcy," he says, "if that's really your name and you're not just trying to be funny," he says, "the last thing you look like is a poet, Darcy! What you *do* look like is somebody from a Acme."

I do not look like a poet. What does a poet look like. Is there a recognized uniform? Has literature evolved a sumptuary paradigm out of its two thousand-plus years of tradition? Oh, they *look* like poets!

Prinslow looks like a poet. He seldom cuts his hair, appears to very seldom wash it, surely never combs or brushes the tangled mop that covers his ears, hangs over his low forehead, dangles before his eyes. Am I no poet because my hair is sculptor-cut, trimmed biweekly, shampooed, blow-dried, and fixed in place with mildly scented spray each morning?

Prinslow, the others who assert they are poets, they all dress the part! Prinslow presents his Fine Arts Center reading of anti-sonnets shirtless, wears only a cracked and stained leather vest to display the grizzled hair on his scrawny chest. His bleached denims are ragged, pocked with tears and holes, held up with a greasy rope. Sockless, his shower-clog sandals flap and snap as he walks to and from the lectern to the reflexive applause of the small audience. His bare feet are dirty, fingernails bitten to the quick, fingers discolored by chain-smoking, teeth in need of prophylaxis—I must not forget his beard, for they almost all affect facial hair!

Prinslow's is a gray-flecked swath he surely trims to keep a short, dingy smear obscuring his lips. Nesbitt, whom I met at the annual convention of the Associated Writing Programs in San Diego last year, hides a weak chin and bad complexion behind a growth full as any hermit's, and Kirkbride, whose latest chapbook is a slim gathering of erotic lyrics cast in the prosody of the limerick, decorates himself with a large Fu Manchu. Moon, who flaunts his sexual preference, sports a cookie duster like Hitler's or Chaplin's, perches granny glasses on the tip of his long nose.

The women—the women who inform me they are poets— are no different. Dawn Ziegler, dressed like a gypsy, all scarves and clanging bracelets and beaded headband, projects the aura of a bag ladies' séance when she declaims the verses she swears come to her only when she is fully immersed in a trance state. China Mae Wheaton (a.k.a. Natanga Umziki), shapeless in an oversize dashiki, cultivates an enormous Afro teased to the size of a medicine ball. At the Library of Congress, which awarded her a medallion for continuous distinctive achievement, Winnifred Bersch enjoyed a *succes de scandale* by reciting her found-poems to the accompaniment of a lute, braless in a see-through blouse. Patty Malone, whose forebears emigrated from the Auld Sod 100 years ago, is always attired in army surplus camouflage fatigues appropriate to the pro-I.R.A. chants she snarls at the camera's eye on educational television shows. Stephanie (a.k.a. Stan) Dykstra, who leads a small claque of militant sapphics, naturally prefers blazers, bow ties, a fedora, trousers with a zipper.

They look like poets. Leonard and Linda Seilig, the husband-wife darlings of the academic critics, much admired for the confessional conjugal epics they produce in collaboration, shaved their heads bald as monks', dressed in pastel unisex jumpsuits for the recent *Tonight Show* guest-shot—they *look* like poets!

Poet-In-Residence

Am I, Darcy, not a poet, less a poet, because I own two dozen three-piece suits? Am I no bard simply because my shoes come from Italy, my ties from Savile Row? If my collars button down, may I not still sing? Shall my words lack luster because my sports and leisure wardrobe meets the norms of my country club, my ski lodge at Vail, the Alaskan preserve where I fly annually to stalk the moose and the grizzly? Am I denied vision because my palate responds to French cuisine, uninspired because I prefer brandy and hand-rolled cigars to the dissipation of beer and cannabis? May I not as readily soar with the muse in my Mercedes?

I know what a poet is!

Poetry is discipline. These poets, the pretenders, boast of their casual routines—they scribble their lines on the backs of envelopes, in scruffy portfolios, on the inside covers of matchbooks; they hunt and peck awkwardly on their battered manual typewriters, scrawl with dull pencil stubs, carelessly compose in ballpoint, write with leaky, archaic fountain pens!

Prinslow loves to regale an audience of poetry society dilettantes with anecdotes of his creativity: how he dashed off an obscene anti-triolet on a soggy napkin while sobering up in an all-night diner; how, no pen or pencil at hand, he scratched a metaphor with a safety pin into the surface of a Formica countertop; how he carries a sharp pocketknife on a chain around his neck, prepared to open a vein and write in his own blood, on his own sallow skin, should the exigencies of a flash of insight ever warrant!

Dawn Ziegler has asserted in print that her semicoherent streams of consciousness are recorded by a kind of automatic writing, her hand and fingers quite beyond her control, that the real work of poetic composition is for her the labor of deciphering the holograph that comes unbidden to her from the fourth dimension. Nesbitt plays shamelessly to crowds, autographs and gives away the messy manuscript copies of his poems he reads from, empties the soiled, tattered folder he lugs to the platform—instant personal souvenirs of his sensibility, he calls them! Winnifred Bersch clips newspapers and magazines, sticks these excerpts to sheets of yellow legal paper, has no need to write, ever, when scissors and library paste serve so well!

"You write your poems on *what*?" exclaims Prinslow.

"A personal computer," I repeat, "a word processor. I tried three or four, but I prefer the Epson, simply because the file commands are so user-friendly."

"Now I know you're having me on, man! Darcy, did you say your name was?"

"Darcy," I tell him, "Poet-In-Residence at Acme."

Poetry is discipline. I am at my desk, in my office suite at Acme's headquarters complex, no later than 8 A.M. five days a week—discipline. Mrs. Licke, my executive assistant, takes my jacket, brings me a cup of black coffee; I unbutton my vest, turn back my cuffs, loosen the knot in my tie, and go to work. Mrs. Licke takes my calls in her office, arranges my afternoon calendar, monitors my coffee cup, replenishes it unobtrusively, and I work. Discipline!

The mechanics may vary. Discipline! Most often, I simply slip a fresh disk in my Epson, give the new file a title—*Labor Contract Negotiations Prose-Poem, Production Control Sestina, Aubade for Middle-Management Breakfast Seminar, Fiscal Year Goals and Objectives: Assorted Epigrams,* etc.—and begin to write. My concentration is unbroken; the air-conditioning sighs, my Epson clicks and hums and beeps, I note the occasional wink of the light on my telephone that tells me Mrs. Licke is vigilant in her protection of my privacy. A poet is one who writes poetry. I write.

I do not loll about, waiting for some ineffable nuance of light or sound to kick-start me into words that may or may not fuse into profundity or sublimity. I do not record the minutia of my every sentient moment, keep no journal to mine like a miser's hoard when my flow of language slows to a trickle, dries. I keep no tape recorder at my bedside in the faint hope my subconscious will generate some surreal dream I can wake to catch hold of before it evaporates like morning dew. I need not peruse every available newspaper or periodical or arcane text to glean the unself-conscious irony of a typesetter's gaffe I can retail to some fugitive literary quarterly. I do not befuddle myself with alcohol or cannabis or runic self-hypnosis to produce a second sight sufficient to create a poem. I work, I write—discipline!

"Mr. Darcy?" whispers Mrs. Licke, crossing the carpeting on tiptoe.

"No more coffee just now, thank you, Mrs. Licke."

"Sir," says she, "Mr. Borger's calling. I have him on hold in my office."

"He knows I write in the morning."

"Yes sir. I reminded him, but it's apparently quite urgent. Something concerned with the media release for the takeover."

"All right," I say, "put him through. But let him cool on hold a couple of minutes before you connect us. He may be Chairman of the Board, but I'm Poet-In-Residence and he knows I write in the mornings."

"Yes, sir," says Mrs. Licke, "I told him you were writing, Mr. Darcy, but he did insist it was urgent."

Interruptions delay me, but I am not long diverted. I do not throw up my hands in despair when the world intrudes; I do not call it a day, pack it in, give myself over to any chance, unavoidable digression; I do not say to myself: the hell with it, Darcy, let it go, there's always tomorrow!

I halt my work, deal with Borger, or Hack, or Biggs, any of

the executives in echelons exalted enough to presume to demand instant audience, and then I go back to work, at my Epson, throughout the remainder of the morning hours.

On the rare occasion when I am blocked—any poet will come up against a block now and then!—I do not surrender. I turn off my Epson, resort to systematic brainstorming, free associating in longhand on a memo blank until I have clarified my intention, designed my strategy, enumerated my tactics, rediscovered, as it were, my poetic voice.

My personalized memo blanks bear an embossed heading:
From the Desk of Robert Darcy
Poet-In-Residence
Acme, Inc.

"I suppose," I tell them, "it depends on your definition of what a poet is."

"A poet," Prinslow says, toying with his pocketknife, "is somebody who's too much alive to write in traditional forms. A *real* poet," he says, "is someone who goes beyond the conventional definitions, man! That's why I write anti-poems. I'm actually an anti-poet. Darcy, did you say your name was?"

"A poet," Moon tells me, cookie duster twitching like a fat black caterpillar as he speaks, "has to express himself or herself in order to fully become what he or she is because society won't let him or her be what they are."

"A poet," says Dawn Ziegler, bracelets clanging as she gestures, rings catching highlights, "is a person with a special gift. I have this gift. I don't understand why I was chosen, but I was chosen to communicate with the Other Side. My mission in life is to mediate between the two planes of existence. A poet is like a conduit, a kind of spiritual pipeline for people who weren't given my gift."

"A poet," says Natanga Umziki (a.k.a. China Mae Wheaton),

"is a culture-giver. Without poets, the masses wouldn't have any humanizing culture; they'd be just so many more animals in the jungle of life. Poets reconnect people to their heritage."

"A poet," says Winnifred Bersch, bending forward, exposing her cleavage, "has to be able to shut off her intellect. Poetry is the result of the emotions' revolt against the cold tyranny of reason. If I walked around *thinking* all day," she says, thrusting her pelvis up and out for emphasis, "I'd never find the found-poems you can find anywhere if you know how to look! Call me Winnie, Darcy," she adds.

Ignorance. Misinformation. Myth. Fallacy. Heresy! I know what a poet is—I am Poet-In-Residence at Acme! A poet needs to *know* things.

A poet needs to know Adam Smith and Karl Marx, Maynard Keynes and Milton Friedman, supply-side and monetarism, balance-of-trade and cash-flow and price-earnings ratios, the foci where automation and worker productivity collide, the crossroads where inflation cancels out real earnings, the byzantium of hierarchical boardroom politics and the nitty-gritty trenches of production control and processing, the delicate equations of raw materials and transportation costs, the cabala of prime rates and discounts, the rat's mazes of administrative structure and regulatory agencies, diversification's risks measured against divestiture's hedge, the balancing act of executive compensation: perquisites, stock options, benefits, base salary, the personality metamorphoses all along the axis from Whiz Kid at one end to Premature Burn-out at the other, the euphoria of three-martini expense-account luncheons contrasted with the migraine that comes of hours-long conference calls, the herd psychology of stockholders, the *a priori* and *post facto* existence of government oversight and cost-plus contracting, tax write-offs and spurious shelters, hard liabilities and de-

ferred penalties, the blue-sky dreams of research and development, the tangled filigree of confidential negotiations conducted
in the limelight of public image and consumer outrage, the
carrot of bonus stock-option incentives and the rod of letting
the chips of responsibility fall where they may—the nuts and
bolts of here and now, the pie-in-the-sky bye and bye, the Yin
and Yang of monopoly's seduction, the trendy drifts of fashion,
the fathomless mystery of failure, the eternal optimism of ambition, the fission of human energy and the entropy of metal
fatigue . . . and all the infinite whole of it manifest in words, and
the impossibility of literal translation. . . .

I tell them: "My name is Darcy. I'm Poet-In-Residence at
Acme, and I tell you a poet has to *know* some things!" Trade, I
feel like telling them, your M.F.A. in for an M.B.A.!

What do they know? Who reads their poetry? How many
people subscribe to *Poetry* or *The Hudson Review,* much less *The
Unspeakable Visions of the Individual* or *Kayak* or *Nimrod*? How
many subscribers peruse the pages; how many decorate a coffee
table with the current quarter's issue?

Read, I feel like telling them. *Time* and *Newsweek* and *U.S.
News & World Report;* read *The Christian Science Monitor* and
The New York Times and *Barron's* and *The Wall Street Journal*
and *Kiplinger's*! Read annual reports and corporate house organs and trade journals! Read intraoffice and interdepartmental
memoranda, technical reports and manuals, read the doodles
left behind in conference rooms when the board adjourns, read
the graffiti in lavatories designated for salaried personnel, piece
together and read the fragments in the shredder's bin!

Read the eyes of a fair-haired boy to learn how much of him
is zeal, how much unexamined self-confidence, how much pure
bluff; read the clamped lips of a comptroller as he hovers over
the bottom line; read the dying spark in the wrinkled visage of

an old corporate war-horse who knows everyone knows he knows early retirement severance is in the offing.

Study is prayer. Learning is sacred. Knowledge is power. Poetry is a way of knowing that which transcends knowing!

I ask them: "Whom do you write your poetry *for*? Define your audience."

"We write," Leonard Seilig says, "for people who share our sensibilities."

"We write," Linda Seilig says, taking her husband's hand, "for people who want to achieve a total bonding with another, the way we have."

"I write," says Stan (a.k.a. Stephanie) Dykstra, "for all my sisters out there, wherever, who need the forum of my poetry to declare their rage and their solidarity, and the joy they feel when they break their shackles!"

"I write," Nesbitt says, inscribing the dog-eared manuscript of his "Sensitive Man Feeling the Dark with His Raw Nerve-Ends: A Haiku" for me—*for Bob Darcy, with the sincere wish there were more of us!*—"because I'm a man with deep feelings and serious ideas, and because I like to think there's a few fellow souls out there, like yourself, Darcy," he says, presenting me with my personal souvenir of his sensibility, "who respond to the same vibes. I think that about says it pretty much for all poets, don't you think?"

No, I do not! I know my audience!

I write for Borger, Chairman of the Board, Acme, Inc., the free world's highest paid executive! Everyone recognizes his name and face—the featured guest four times last year on *Meet the Press,* twice on *Face the Nation,* interviewed up close and personal by Barbara Walters. He weekends frequently at Camp David, golfs at Burning Tree with a foursome of Supreme Court justices, gets his briefings on international developments straight from Henry the K., hired Perlman to play "Because" and "I Love You Truly" on the fiddle at his daughter's wedding when she married her first marquis—I, Darcy, write for J. J. Borger!

Says he: "I don't recognize the meter you've given me, Darcy, I don't feel comfortable reciting these lines."

"Work at it, Mr. Borger," I tell him. "It's called Skeltonics. You want to convey force, conviction, vigor, determination, don't you?"

"You know I do. The President's going to be there, along with half the foreign diplomatic corps in D.C. If I come off at all like I'm waffling, we can kiss this takeover goodbye."

"There's no hesitation in Skeltonics," I tell him. "The alliterations give you snap, crackle, pop! The short line shows you know exactly where you're headed, and nobody's about to stop you. Trust me!" I tell Borger, Chairman of the Board of Acme, Inc.

"I'd better," he says, "you're the poet here." He is J. J. Borger, and everyone recognizes the meringue-pie hair, the grandfather's eyes twinkling behind the gold-framed spectacles, the tan-rosy chubby cheeks, the merry mouth that reveals just the edge of his very sharp, very white teeth when he smiles—I write my poems for *him*!

I write for Biggs, Vice-Chairman of the Board, Borger's right hand, the one that holds the hatchet, grasps the strings that open and close the corporate coffers—a long and casual drink of water, this Biggs, but his eyes are reptilian, and he never perspires; his is the hand at Acme that pats the heads of high flyers on their way up, slaps down the upstarts, strokes the aggrieved, prods the lethargic into dynamism, reins in the reckless.

"Darcy," he asks, "why the closed couplets instead of open? It might feel more sincere, natural, if there was more enjambment and less end-stopping."

Poet-In-Residence

"Think about it," I tell him. "You're addressing shareholders, live in the Astrodome and over closed-circuit satellite link to half the civilized world, right? Do they want *casual*? Do they want blank verse that sounds like casual conversation? A loose syntactic line that doesn't even sound like poetry?"

"You tell me Darcy, you're the Poet-In-Residence."

"That I am." I say. "They want *order*! They want neat and tidy, symmetry. They want to hear how they never had it so good, and you're the man up there at the microphone with figures proving just how fast and fat it's coming to them this quarter, right?"

"It's been a good quarter," Biggs allows, "even with the disappointing performance of our new home-computer line."

"Which is where the imagery of the shadow looming behind us in the valley comes in," I explain. "Didn't you catch that darkness leitmotif I worked in in the middle stanzas? The closed couplets work against the shadow images, counterpoint, it gives the necessary tension to let them know you're on top of the situation. See it?"

"If you say so," says Biggs, "but I still feel like I'd sound more leader-like and persuasive with more enjambed lines."

"Why," I ask him, "do you think they call them *heroic* couplets?"

I write my poems for Biggs.

Do I make it sound a bit like Grub Street? Oh no! It is not easy. Poetry is never *easy*! Case in point: I struggle with a villanelle for Hack, Vice-President for Labor Relations, Acme, Inc.

"I *need* your villanelle, Darcy!" he pleads on the telephone.

"You told me," I say. "And I need a little more time for revision, which I told you! Relax, Hack, Mrs. Licke's got the draft I edited this morning on the laser printer right now, but I'm not signing off on it until I'm satisfied."

"Darcy," Hack says, "you know I wouldn't presume to know the first thing about serious literature—"

"Then don't!"

"—but I saw the draft before this one, and it looked okay to me. Darcy? Are you still on the line, Darcy?"

I hold a beat, say, "Hack, you need a poem for the awards ceremony you dreamed up to honor Acme's Production Worker of the Year, right? I propose to deliver you a prosodically regular villanelle, which villanelle you can read aloud at your banquet in front of the cameras, and which villanelle will be engraved in bronze on the walnut plaque you're presenting the awardee along with a certified check in the amount of five thou, right?"

"Please, Darcy," Hack says, "it's tomorrow night!"

"Art," I remind Hack, "won't be rushed. Do you have the foggiest notion, Hack," I ask him, "how tough it is to get a name like *Walkiewicz* to scan?"

I know who my audience is: I write for Borger and Biggs and Hack; I write for Walkiewicz, Acme's Production Worker of the Year; I write for *Acme Musings*—a monthly, translated into nine languages!—I write for the thousands who make up the Acme corporate family of employees, for the millions of Acme customers worldwide! I, Darcy, write for the shakers and movers, the insiders, the technocrats, the paper-shufflers, for anonymous hewers of plastic and drawers of electronic impulses into whose otherwise impenetrable lives the pervasive influence of Acme would extend without palpable presence, unknown because unnamed!

What poet dare hope for, dare dream of, more?

They call themselves *poets*—Prinslow, Nesbitt, Kirkbride, Wheaton-Umziki, and Stan-Stephanie, Linda and Leonard and Winnie (*et alia ad infinitum!*). Poets, they tell me, wait upon the muse, or a chemical's twist in the brain's blood, or a specter's hint, or a random permutation of words to appear! Poets, they tell me, should trash tradition, minister to the oppressed and abnormal, shock the complacent, spin substance from the vacuum! Poets, they tell me, write poems for kindred spirits and soul-fellows, for the downtrodden insensate, because . . .

I do not regard what they tell me!

I *know* what a poet, what poetry, is, why the poet makes poems, whom his poetry serves. Why bother to explain?

Accept the paradox: the poet creates the poem, and the poem creates the microcosm of the poet's choice. The reverse is also true: the cosmos finds itself in the poem, the poem implies its creator—me, who and what I am, what I do—Darcy, Acme's Poet-In-Residence!

IMMEDIATE REVIEW

ℰℐ

> *The academicians in Plato's grove, after much debate, defined man as a featherless biped; this definition was thought sufficient until a citizen plucked a chicken and threw it over the wall into the grove.*
>
> —*apocryphal*

IMMEDIATE REVIEW as described hereinafter is defined as the process whereby middle-management-level personnel in the employ of Unitron, Inc. (to include all subsidiary divisions: Unitech, Unifab, Univend, Uniserve) may elect to bypass established evaluation/ promotion procedures.
—*Unitron Personnel Manual, p. 64*

"If I can trust my understanding of the guidelines, seeing as how this isn't exactly a frequent occasion hereabouts, the nitty-gritty of just how we go at this is pretty much left to my discretion," said Barkley, Leff's Immediate Review Hearing Officer. "Barring objections from either Mr. Leff or his counsel, and unless any member of the committee has anything to inject before we get rolling here . . . Ladies? Gentlemen? Okay, then what I'm going to do is get us in gear with a fairly informal outline of how we'll proceed, after which we'll do just that. Agreed? Ladies? Gentlemen? Mr. Leff?"

"Watch him, Leffie," Witz whispered in Leff's ear, "he's old and he's cranky and he'll probably forget half what's said after we break for lunch, but he's been a company man all his life and he'll stick it to you just on general principles if you let him."

"Agreed," Leff said to Barkley from his end of the conference table, "which is to say I reserve my right to object if we find ourselves getting too far away from the guidelines, okay?"

"I'll just add," Barkley said, "that it's my job as hearing officer to see we don't digress to the point we're counter-productive. That said," Barkley said, nodding to the stenotypist borrowed from Legal, "let's get on the record."

"Mistake!" Witz leaned close to whisper. "Now you've questioned his integrity and got him teed off at you to start!"

While Unitron, Inc. is confident that established procedures are adequate to all personnel situations, the corporation recognizes the possibility of error; IMMEDIATE REVIEW manifests this recognition, providing individuals harboring substantive grievances of a personnel nature the opportunity to attain mutually satisfactory resolutions of such grievances, thus maintaining and enhancing the harmonious relationship between employed and employer necessary to efficient and productive corporate existence.
—Unitron Personnel Manual, p. 66

Leff, Public Relations Specialist Grade III in Unitron's Uniserve Division, had a grievance; the trouble was, he couldn't put his finger on it, couldn't nail it down, set it out in black and white to make the rest of his world see it, rise up, and demand redress on his behalf.

It wasn't exactly money. Leff, 36, was making his age in salary, and the stock options Uniserve offered middle management, though they couldn't compare to the giveaways the boys on bonus row were handed semiannually, endowed his far-distant retirement prospects with at least a rosy tinge, if not a glow.

"It's not just the money, we do okay," he said to his wife, Jill.

"We manage because I manage, Leffie," Jill said. "Leffie, sometimes I think you don't appreciate how I keep this family going. Are you aware how I innovate to cut corners just to dress the girls decently, much less myself, and keep your appearance up to snuff since you're so set on making bonus row?"

"I owe you a lot, Jill," Leff said. "I did say it's not only the money I make."

"Girls are more costly than boys, in case you never thought about it, Leffie," she said, "and I'm only talking about basic expenses. Consider for a second the extras I connive to give them that you don't even probably think about. Joanna's got definite artistic sensibility, but do you have any idea what mime lessons go for these days? Jane's natural grace would be lost to us forever if it weren't for tap and jazz and ballet classes, wouldn't it? Did you know I made the last payment on Jolene's bassoon this month? Did you know Janet's got her heart set on trying out for cheerleading when she gets to junior high? That means gymnastics training, Leffie!"

Leff said, "At least Joyce's too young to sign up for anything yet."

"You're so oblivious, Leffie!" his wife said. "I enrolled her this week in Arts for Tots—you have to discover children's talents early to exploit them, Leffie! And what appreciation do I get for making all this possible on your salary?"

"I said I owe you," he said.

"Complain!" Jill said. "A lovely home and five lovely, gifted daughters, a wife who looks after everything so you can pursue your career, and your nose is out of joint because you're not up on bonus row with the big shots yet like your pal Witz!"

"It's not the money. It's part that and part of a lot of things I can't exactly say," Leff said, but Jill had left the room, calling to their daughters to get ready, it was time to pile into the station wagon and get to their lessons.

Immediate Review

It was *not* money! Jill *was* a whiz with the household finances, and Leff always had money in his wallet for middle-management-cafeteria lunches, never lacked a buck to play office pools, always had five to kick in when a secretary married or had a baby, could afford to spring for a round of drinks when he and Witz stopped off at the Sans Souci on the way home after a long day, never put his hand in his pocket without hearing the ring of quarters and dimes. Although it rankled him that his wife still mended his socks and turned his shirt collars and saved plastic bags and clipped shopping coupons, it was not so much the big jump in salary that came up on bonus row Leff wanted.

> *Personnel contemplating the submission of a formal request for IMMEDIATE REVIEW are strongly urged to first consider the implications of such action; while a favorable recommendation rendered by the duly appointed Hearing Committee does, in accordance with policies articulated herein, automatically bestow the desired promotion and/or salary increment increase, should the Committee render a recommendation, sustaining the existing personnel evaluation of the aggrieved, corporation policy as articulated herein dictates the immediate termination (without forfeiture of severance compensation and other relevant contractual benefits) of the aggrieved. Thus, IMMEDIATE REVIEW should be considered only in instances wherein personnel concerned have, after careful deliberation, determined a specific and tangible grievance may be said to prevail.*
> —Unitron Personnel Manual, p. 67

"I think we all know each other's names," Barkley said, "and I'm not backing off from what I said about keeping this relaxed. Still, I think for the official record we should all introduce ourselves. I'll begin. I'm Sherman Barkley, and I've been designated by Personnel to conduct Mr. Leff's immediate review in the capacity of hearing officer, which capacity I take to mean chair of this committee, and I'll add until most recently, I was

Public Relations Specialist Grade VII with Mr. Leff's division, Uniserve. Presently, as PR liaison attached to the board of directors, I troubleshoot situations such as this one. I see my responsibility as keeping us on track with policy and procedure guidelines as set forth in our manual."

"I told you he was ticked off, Leffie," Witz whispered. "Catch the umbrage in his tone? We're going to hear him cite his authority and his long years of loyal service from here on. Make a point of deferring to him, Leffie. I've seen him operate—he digs getting his dignity greased!"

"I'm Simon Forrest," said the man to Barkley's left. "I've been with Unitron for 21 years plus. I started in what they're calling Uniserve now before it had a name, and then I went to Unitech when we made the big push for research and development." Forrest paused to swallow and tamp his pipe, then said, "I'm a Research Coordinator Grade IV, so I'm thoroughly familiar with evaluation and appraisal from almost every angle."

Witz leaned over. "Forrest's a notorious dud, Leffie," he said, sotto voce. "Word I get is they bumped him up and out of Uniserve rather than sack him because they thought he'd croak of nervous collapse if they gave him walking papers."

"Can we trust him for a fair shake?" Leff asked.

"Not in the picture," Witz said. "You have to realize he's not capable of independent thought. He'll flop whichever way Barkley leans."

"My name is Nadine Archibald," said the young woman seated to Barkley's right. "I'm sure I'm junior here," she said and laughed. "And I'll confess up front this is my first exposure to this sort of thing, since I'm so new to Unitron. I represent Univend Division, and I'm a Consumer Analyst Grade II."

Witz wrote on his yellow pad and nudged it in front of Leff on the conference table: *Affirmative action sop!* Leff looked at Nadine Archibald. Her haircut reminded him of the barbering done on Marine Corps recruits; enormous earrings dangled close to the padded shoulders of her jacket; though her eyelashes were black with mascara, she wore no lipstick or nail polish; when she smiled at Leff he saw her very small, very sharp teeth.

Try charm! Witz reached over to write on Leff's yellow pad. Leff smiled at her, resisted an impulse to wink.

"Bill Paxson here," said the man next to Nadine Archibald. "Unifab," he said. He had removed his jacket before he took his seat at the conference table, revealing a row of gleaming mechanical pencils in the breast pocket of his white shirt. "Engineering Supervisor Grade III," Bill Paxson said. His jacket off, he had methodically turned back his cuffs; his forearms were hairy and muscular, fingers short and blunt. His Adam's apple was prominent, his jaw jutted, his brow smooth and broad as a block of whitewashed stone, and his small eyes looked at Leff as if he were a messy blueprint.

"Problem solver?" Leff whispered to Witz.

"Robot," Witz muttered.

There was a long silence before the last member of the committee, who was bent over his yellow pad, writing rapidly, realized it was his turn to speak. He looked up when Sherman Barkley cleared his throat. "Oops!" he said. "Sorry. I was jotting a reminder to myself about some topics I wanted to bring up when the time comes. I'm Peter Klimp, and like Miss Archibald here—"

"*Ms.* Archibald!" Nadine Archibald said.

"—oops! Sorry," Peter Klimp said. "Anyway, I'm also pretty much virgin when it comes to evaluation and appraisal, but I welcome this opportunity to learn the ropes, as it were."

They waited for him to continue, but he lowered his head, resumed writing on his pad, the scratch of his pencil the only sound in the conference room. "Peter," Barkley said, "will you state your job classification and your division for the steno-typist?"

"Huh?" Peter Klimp said, looking up. "Oh. Oops and sorry once more! Chemist Grade VI. Unitech. I work with polymers." He resumed writing.

Grade 6! Leff wrote on his pad. Whiz kid? Intelligent, trained in logical thought—insight on issues?

"Scientist," Witz hissed softly. "He diddles with equations, Leffie, not people's lives and careers!"

"Good," Sherman Barkley said. "Now I'll ask Mr. Witz to state his name and job title for our record, and maybe sketch in his sense of function here as Mr. Leff's counsel or advocate or whatever you like, and then we'll kick off with Mr. Leff's presentation of his bill of particulars. Okay with all concerned?"

Simon Forrest lit his pipe with a series of strangulated sucking noises; Nadine Archibald seemed, to Leff, to hood her eyes and make a kissing shape with her bloodless lips; Bill Paxson nodded once; Peter Klimp put a period at the end of a sentence, underscored a word twice, then looked up, nodded vigorously, as if his head had become unhinged.

"What have I got to lose?" Leff mumbled to Witz.

"Everything," his counsel said. "Leffie, I think we're up the proverbial creek with this crew! What's Forrest smoke in that pipe, yak hair?"

The burden of proof lies with the aggrieved, who shall be afforded every opportunity in the course of his/her IMMEDIATE REVIEW to enumerate, elaborate, and establish for the information of the Committee's members, the full and complete particulars of his/her grievance.
—Unitron Personnel Manual, p. 70

"So if it ain't the bucks we're talking here," Witz said, "then what is it's got you uptight, Leffie?"

"I think," Leff said, "I'm beginning to feel like I don't make any difference with my work. I don't make anything happen."

"Jeffrey! Hit us again, same way," Witz called out to the bartender. "Make *what* happen?" he said to Leff.

"Nothing. Anything. Everything," Leff said, drained the dregs of his gimlet, set the glass aside on the shimmering bartop to make room for the next round.

"Leffie," Witz said, putting money on the bar, "you go into Immediate Review with nothing but mid-life crisis, I promise you you'll wind up at the front gate with your severance check in your hand."

What grieved him, Leff thought as he sipped his fresh gimlet, stared at himself in the Sans Souci's smoky backbar mirror, scanned the labels on the racks of bottles arrayed on glass shelves beneath the mirror, was partly his intensifying aware- ness that he, Leff, Public Relations Specialist Grade III, was simply not . . . not a *force* in the massive, intricate matrix of Unitron, Inc. He initiated nothing, altered nothing; he was wholly other-directed, his role in the function of Uniserve Divi- sion analogous to a walk-on in the cast of a crowd scene. He was, Leff felt, utterly without influence on the job.

"I'm a corporate flunky," he told Witz at the Sans Souci's attitude adjustment hour. "A factotum. Supernumerary."

Leff was invited to PR campaign strategy sessions, but never delivered the presentations, was seldom asked his opinion. Ex- pected to take copious notes, to write voluminous summaries of his notes, he felt an aura of indulgent exasperation from the group if he requested a point of clarification. He wrote meticu- lous copy drafts but could not recognize his words when edited proofs came back from Printing. If he was valued, it was only for his precise grasp of grammar, his plodder's facility in spotting the misplaced comma, the sentence fragment, the printer's typo.

Messengers dropped sheaves of manuscript, folders crammed with editorial queries, blocks of perfect-bound galleys in his office cubicle; messengers—faceless, sexless, anonymous in their burnt orange Uniserve smocks—came to his cubicle to retrieve the oversize envelopes and rubber-banded stacks of work he turned out like a production-line machine. Yet none of this, Leff knew—not his energy nor his intelligence, his commonsense know-how nor his experience—made the faintest discernible impact on Uniserve's unceasing public relations mission.

"I want to be able to say to myself, *I make a difference,*" he told Witz in the Sans Souci.

"And you think you would up on bonus row, is that it?" Witz said. "Think again. It's more of the same, just with more bucks and the perks. Take it from the horse's mouth, Leffie."

"I want to count for something," Leff said.

"Dreamer," Witz said. "Can you stand one more?"

"I've got to go," Leff said. "If I buy another round I won't be able to afford lunch tomorrow. Besides, Jill gets supper early tonight. My kid's performing in a bassoon opera or something."

"Jeffrey! Just one this time," Witz called. "Anyhow," he said to Leff, "enjoy your dinner, try not to torture yourself about bonus row, huh, pal?"

"Leftovers," Leff said. "It's only partly feeling like I don't have any effect on anything."

The IMMEDIATE REVIEW Committee shall be furnished all relevant documentary evidence, and such documentation shall, as a matter of course, be shared with both the aggrieved and his/her designated Counsel-Advocate.
—*Unitron Personnel Manual, p. 72*

"My name is Elroy Percival Witz," Witz said. "I'm Public Relations Specialist Grade IV. I'm here at Leffie's—Mr. Leff's

request and invitation. I suppose for background I should say
we're friends. We came to Unitron—to Uniserve Division—at
about the same time. What is it, Leffie, nine, ten years now?"

"Eleven almost," Leff said.

"Eleven," Witz said. "How time flies when you're having fun,
huh?" he said to the committee, paused, went on when nobody
laughed except Leff. "Up until some six months ago he and I
worked almost in tandem, coauthored proposals, edited each
other's copy, at least informally, attended the same staff confer-
ences, were assigned to a lot of the same tactical teams, campaign task forces, you get the idea."

"Until he was promoted to bonus row," Leff said.

"I'm still with Uniserve, but I moved over to the division
admin staff, so we don't relate on the job anymore."

"*Up!*" Leff said. "They moved him *up* to Grade IV, to bonus
row, and I got left behind, passed over for the second time,
where I still am, where I think they'll let me sit and rot until I
retire, which is why I demanded Immediate Review!"

"But we're still friends," Witz said to the committee, then
turned to his friend. "Leffie, just wait until it's your turn to talk
okay, buddy?"

"Amen," Sherman Barkley said; Simon Forrest, pipe in mouth,
nodded assent; Nadine Archibald showed her small, sharp
teeth; Bill Paxson stared, unblinking, through Leff at the conference room wall behind him; Peter Klimp scribbled on his
yellow pad; the stenographer from Legal, eyes closed to concentrate, sat with her legs crossed, her long fingers poised over the
stenograph machine's keys.

When he began to feel as if the seat of his pants was annealed
to the plastic-covered cushion of his chair, to feel as if the pangs
that started in the small of his back were mounting his spine,
threatening to bloom at the base of his skull, flood his brain

with a migraine, Leff decided to risk a personal call on the division circuit. He looked away from the laser-print copy that danced before his eyes like a seismograph's stylus, but there was really nothing to see from his cubicle. Whichever way he turned, Leff saw the reflective glass walls that split Uniserve's PR copy department into cells like a beehive, an anthill, the dens of a rat warren. When he closed his eyes, massaged his throbbing temples, tried to listen, he heard only a fog of sound; the liquid clack of computer keyboards, the feral growl of ventilation, random pockets of subdued modulated voices in earnest discussion. When he began to feel he would scream, Leff grabbed his desk phone and punched out Witz's unlisted extension on the button.

As the receiver buzzed in his ear, he lofted an unspoken prayer that Cost Control's monitors would not be on his department's case this day, checking phone logs—all Leff needed, he thought, was to be called in to alibi unauthorized communication!

"Witz here," Witz said, his voice sounding very distant, remote, more bass in it—as if he spoke, not from his office in divisional admin's blue complex, but from a great height, the executive penthouse on Uniserve's roof, the peak of a mountain in a foreign land.

"It's Leffie," Leff said. "Speak to me, Witz. Say something real and personal so I'll know I'm alive or awake and not having a bad dream."

"Cute," Witz said. "Should you be doing this? Cost Control never sleeps, they say, right? You don't get to bonus row abusing communications, Leffie. This is getting to be a bad habit. Okay, so what can I do you for, or is this one just to bitch again about your cruel fate?"

"Meet me in front of the main gate when we knock off," Leff said, "I'll treat you at the Sans Souci."

"You treated yesterday. Seriously, Leffie," Witz said, "I'd like to, but no can do. I've got a retreat."

"A *which?*"

"Retreat. It's a thing in admin, somebody's new wrinkle. That's admin for you, Leffie. Once a month, the new people take our elevator up to the penthouse at five o'clock. Drinks. Snacks. Motivational films, slide-shows, lectures. They say it makes for more cohesive identity. It runs a couple hours, then we all take a sauna together and a dip in the pool and go home."

"Never heard of it before," Leff said.

"No reason you should have," Witz said. "*I* never heard of it until I made bonus row. It's a perk, Leffie."

"It figures."

"So. Sorry. Maybe tomorrow? Hang up now, Leffie, Cost Control's probably tracing down your extension right this minute."

"I'll call you tomorrow and remind you."

"No, I'll call *you!* I'm the one with the unmonitored, unlimited-call extension, remember?" Witz hung up.

Part of what grieved him, Leff decided, was the perks.

When he drove into Unitron's parking mall #D-4, Leff had to roll down his window, insert a card with a metallic strip in a slot to raise the barrier; Witz and the others on bonus row were cheerfully waved past a guardhouse by uniformed security. Leff trudged a block and a half through a dank concrete tunnel to his elevator; Witz's personal parking space was stenciled with his name—*Mr. Witz*—and he rode an automated shuttle to division admin's blue lobby. Leff ducked into his cubicle, expected to work at his desk with his jacket on, tie snugged up tight; bonus row handed their suitcoats to secretary-receptionists to hang for them, opened their collars, rolled up their sleeves. Leff wore his plastic name tag—*Leff,* the burnt orange of Uniserve—throughout the working day; in admin, Witz was greeted by name. Leff carried his burnt orange tray in the line at the mid-management cafeteria, paid a cashier, scanned the long, bare tables for a clean spot to sit and eat; bonus row dined in the soft blue decor of admin's restaurant at round cloth-covered tables seating no more than four, meals chosen from a menu, orders taken by blue-clad waitresses who wore high heels and net stockings.

Leff had to descend one floor in his elevator to use a lavatory, which, though clean, was large enough to serve an airport. His invitation to the annual Unitron spring picnic was posted on the department's bulletin board amidst the notices urging productivity and cost control, exhorting morale and team spirit. His copy of *Unitron Musings* came in the in-house mail drop. He signed in and out with a grease pencil, wrote his destination and probable time of return on a huge, clear-plastic overlay sheet. Quitting time for mid-management at Uniserve was announced by a set of chimes like the ones summoning a floor-walker in a department store, a series of flashing blips on the screens of all the computer terminals.

Witz enjoyed a private toilet with shower stall in his office, a paid-up country club membership, a personal secretary he could instruct to hold his calls, and a WATS line option on his extension! The elevator he rode played soothing mood music in stereo.

"Yeah," Leff told Witz the next time they hit the Sans Souci, "you could say it's partly the perks I want."

"Mostly eyewash, Leffie," Witz said. "I know it looks like fat city from where you sit, but it's more illusion than reality, honest."

"Then maybe what I want's some illusion," Leff said, "something I can believe in even if it's not real."

IMMEDIATE REVIEW, perhaps more so than any circumstance arising in the context of corporate operations, requires for its successful conduct the expression of all points of view with unmitigated

candor; all concerned are urged to strive for a frank and direct mode
of communication.
                                    —*Unitron Personnel Manual, p. 81*

Bound copies of Leff's semiannual Personnel Performance
Efficiency Appraisal reports lay on the conference table before
each committee member. Beside him at his end of the table,
Witz thumbed the pages of his copy, making a clucking noise
with his tongue. Leff's original copy, foxed and dog-eared, lay
unopened next to his yellow note pad.

"I'll focus on productivity," Bill Paxson said, looking through
him at the wall. "I don't find citation of a single solitary PR
campaign proposal authored or coauthored, which, if accurate,
I think's appalling over the course of eleven years in your
position."

"Authorship gets lost in the shuffle," Leff said. "Not a proposal goes to the board I didn't contribute to. Others develop
my concepts, or I edit final drafts. My role doesn't show. I don't
suck up to the right parties to get my byline on what the board
sees."

"Leffie—Mr. Leff isn't the sort to blow his own horn near
hard enough."

"I quote," Simon Forrest said without removing his smolder-
ing pipe from his mouth, "'Productivity appraisal: satisfactory.'
Unquote. Both occasions when you were passed over for so-
called bonus row."

"What I don't see in all this is evidence of original or innova-
tive participation," Peter Klimp said without looking up from
Leff's reports. "Over at Unitech, you don't come up with pat-
ents you're out the door, but maybe that's a function of research
and development. Maybe I don't understand Uniserve's mission
adequately?"

"Unitech develops. Unifab makes. Univend sells," Leff said.
"Uniserve tells all about it."

"Leffie's no slouch when it comes to brainstorming, folks!" Witz said.

"I'm the one who came up with the 'We Put *You* In Unitron!' slogan," Leff said. "Two years ago? It was on all the networks, but you won't find any credit for it there."

"Be that as it may," Sherman Barkley said, "I'd like to turn our attention to the narrative sections of these reports."

"Those are subjective in the extreme, everyone knows that," Leff said.

"I quote," Simon Forrest said, exhaling a miasma of pipe smoke, "'Mr. Leff seems to prefer working in isolation. While he is reliable and diligent in carrying out specific assigned tasks, he appears unwilling to engage in the intense interpersonal relationships so vital to departmental mission performance.' Unquote."

"I don't even know what that says in plain English," Leff said.

"You don't work well with others?" Peter Klimp suggested.

"It means in a corporation you have to interface," said Bill Paxson.

"It says to me you're not a team player," Sherman Barkley said, "and it also can be taken to reflect on your basic loyalty to your employer."

"If I may," Nadine Archibald said, eyes bright, teeth flashing, "I'd like to ask about some of these items listed under 'Additional Personal Observations.'"

"That's the category they use when they can't find a *real* reason to zap you!" Leff said.

"I'd hoped we could zero in on tangibles?" Witz said.

"It says here, more than once," she said, "you tell ethnic anecdotes in the cafeteria. Are there any women, blacks, or persons of unorthodox sexual preference in your department, Mr. Leff?"

Leff grieved. He grieved for Jill, his wife, because her life had become an unending struggle to make ends meet, a dizzying quest to create petty sparks of beauty and promise in the lives of their children because there were none in hers, none in his. Leff grieved for his five daughters, because their lives were filled with the trivia of culture: plastic and graphic arts, dance, music, *mime*—because their parents would not or could not generate a human center for them to live in and by. He grieved because his life's work was a white-collar peonage in service to an entity so vast and complicated its identity boggled his imagination when he tried to conceive it. He grieved because there was no coherent relationship between the regimen of his efforts and their obscure effects, because the sea of rhetoric in which he floundered to stay afloat, the pit of words into which he tumbled each day when he entered his cubicle, would never yield a name for the purpose of—or the just reward for—his existence.

Leff grieved because . . . because he was Leff, and he needed something to tell him what that meant, that there was virtue if not value inherent and implicit in what he was or could be or even only might have been!

"I'm doing it!" Leff told his wife.

"You're worse than naive, Leffie," Jill said. "You're a fool! You're going to endanger everything I've worked to make possible for you, for me, for our children. Are you so bent on self-destruction, Leffie?" she asked, and almost wept.

"If I am," he said, "at least it's something I can understand."

The IMMEDIATE REVIEW Committee shall consider no detail, no nuance of possibly relevant input to be beyond the scope of its inquiry; inquiry appropriate to IMMEDIATE REVIEW must be definitive and comprehensive.

—Unitron Personnel Manual, p. 84

Bill Paxson said, "You don't carry a pen or pencil or a note-book, I notice. How do you keep track of things when they come to your attention on the job?"

Simon Forrest said, "I quote. 'Mr. Leff's demeanor fails to exhibit that air of confident positivism typical of higher-level corporate management and administration.'"

Peter Klimp said, "Okay, your job's to tell the world about Unitron. I work with polymer compounds over at Unitech, so tell me a for-instance of what you'd tell the President of the United States about Unitron's leadership in polymers. Or is that too technical?"

Nadine Archibald said, "I'm curious to ask if you think a person has a responsibility to society outside her or his job respon-sibility. Have you ever marched in a protest demonstration, Mr. Leff? Do you contribute to any progressive political action groups? Did you ever sign a petition demanding anyone's equal rights? I'm asking if you have a social conscience, Mr. Leff."

Witz whispered, "I warned you, Leffie."

"Will you or won't you?"

"You know I will, Leffie," Witz had said. "I'm just trying to get you to consider the fallout if you lose. Have you thought about your wife and those five adorable little hostages to for-tune, friend?"

"I'm thinking of them, at least in part. I need to do it to earn their respect."

"Leffie, what's to respect if you get chopped?"

"If not theirs, then mine."

"Leffie, from what I gather nosing around, it's been since Adam was a corporal that anyone asked for it, and longer than that since someone won. Rumor is, the last guy who got the automatic promotion woke up doing market analysis surveys in Yemen or Oklahoma, I forget which."

"Will you or not?"

"I will," Witz said. "I just want you to know I think it's senseless."

"It makes sense to stand up for yourself when you're not treated fair."

"Who says everything's fair? I'm on bonus row, you're not— so where's fair?"

"I forget who said it. Me. *I* say: A man has to be counted."

"For sure—as in nine, ten, you're out."

"At least I can say I was counted," Leff said.

The aggrieved shall, throughout the process of IMMEDIATE RE-VIEW, be afforded every opportunity to respond to any and all allegations, however frivolous.
      —*Unitron Personnel Manual, p. 89*

Sherman Barkley said, "What do you say to charges that a person I won't name found some doodles on scrap paper in your wastebasket—a cartoon of our Unitron logo making it look like a swastika, and also the phrase, 'Unitron Puts It To *You!*'?"

"Hearsay!" Witz said. "Don't answer, Leffie!"

"A person," Leff said, "has a right to his private thoughts, even if it's on company time, for example when you're on hold on your extension or it's three minutes to five, too late to start anything new!"

Simon Forrest said, "Your personal grooming is described by several of your colleagues as casual at best, shabby at worst."

"My wife cuts my hair with a home haircutting kit," Leff said. "If she didn't, and if she didn't turn my collars and darn my socks, I couldn't afford cafeteria lunches or cultural betterment for the next generation of my family!"

Bill Paxson said, "You're known to frequent the premises of a public establishment vending strong spirits—are you an alcoholic, Mr. Leff? You also make calls of a personal nature on your office extension—that's documented by Cost Control!"

"Hold on there!" Witz said. "Name me a dozen names all across bonus row don't bend the elbow now and again, at least socially!"

"It says somewhere drink not only water, have some wine once in a while," Leff said. "I like the Sans Souci's indirect lighting, and Jeffrey's a friendly barkeep even if he does get snotty sometimes, and by the third gimlet I can forget myself!"

Peter Klimp said, "How do you reply to the contention you're mediocre, Leff? You're interchangeable—fungible, we call it in chemistry—a dime a dozen on the job market? How long do you think you'd last in my lab?"

"Can we at least retain civility?" Witz asked.

Nadine Archibald said, "Are you a chauvinist, Mr. Leff? You're obviously Caucasian. Are you also of Anglo-Saxon derivation? Is your religious background Protestant? Which side did you root for during Watergate?"

"I'm *me!*" Leff shouted, stood up at his end of the table, threw off Witz's restraining hand. "*Leff!* Public Relations Specialist Grade III! PR copy department, Uniserve Division, Unitron!" His voice boomed, echoed in the conference room. "Don't you see?" he said. "That's not enough! I'm a drudge, a plodder, a cipher! I lack imagination, my energies flag easily, I drink a little too much a little too often, I suspect I harbor deep-seated bias with respect to numerous minorities! I'm an ineffectual husband and a neglectful parent!"

"Leffie," Witz said, "sit down, Leffie. Please? Take my handkerchief. Wipe your face, blow your nose, huh, old buddy?"

"Don't you really see?" Leff said when he had composed himself. "I'm everything you and these reports say I am, but I still need to be important to somebody! Don't any of you see that?"

Immediate Review

The IMMEDIATE REVIEW Committee's recommendation shall be communicated, immediately upon the close of in camera deliberation, in person to the aggrieved; thereafter, said recommendation will be forwarded to the appropriate division's Personnel Board for implementation of the recommended action.
—*Unitron Personnel Manual, p. 91*

"Mr. Leff," Sherman Barkley said, "it is now my responsibility as hearing officer of this committee to read to you and your counsel-advocate this body's recommendation. I'll add before I read it that we're unanimous. No dissents, no codicils."

Leff looked at the committee members—at Barkley, who rattled the page in his hands; at Forrest, who ground at the bowl of his pipe with a pocketknife; at Paxson, who cleared his throat and checked the count of his mechanical pencils; at Klimp, who sat with his hands folded on the table, eyes half-closed, as if praying or meditating or calculating; at Archibald, who touched two fingertips to her pale lips, as if in affectionate greeting or fond farewell. At his side, he heard Witz catch and hold his breath.

Leff looked at them, waited to hear whether or not—if only in the cosmos that was Unitron, if only in the narrow landscape that was Immediate Review—Leff waited to find out if, in and of himself alone, he, Leff, could be said to matter, waited to hear the current market value of his grief pronounced.

BUNCE'S NEIGHBORS

ℰℐ

> . . . *attention must be paid.*
> —Death of a Salesman

Bunce's house shared a cul-de-sac street with only four others, quiet neighbors—the salesman, Grubgeld, hinted at a secret covenant that kept out *the sort none of us wants in our face,* lawns, thick hedges protecting the windows, a six-foot privacy fence defending each backyard: "A man," Grubgeld said, leering, "could bring it home with him and enjoy it out under the stars, nobody'd care or be the wiser, get my drift? Save you the trouble working the bars, huh? Hey," he said, "slap some drapes and curtains up here, you could plot the revolution in your living room, nobody here's going to know or care!"

There, in his tract house that looked very like the other four on the cul-de-sac in Nottingham Estates, Bunce took up residence, plodded on toward the necessary end so lucidly predicted for him in the data he used to pitch life policies to his indifferent, reluctant, suspicious, sometimes hostile clientele.

And yet . . .

Yet, there *was* one minor distinction in the amorphous mass that was the character of Bunce, one trivial, harmless, worthless trait he had known in himself since childhood. Bunce *noticed* things. He looked, saw, indulged in concerted introspection over perceptions beneath or beyond the interest of most others. He was, Bunce conceded, a kind of casual spy without portfolio, an observer without commission, an instinctive seeker after epiphanies that yielded no significant insights. He had been this way as long as he could remember.

His parents tried to break him of it. When his mother caught him staring at the blocky orthopedic shoe of a cripple who sat near them on a bus—Bunce was no more than six or seven— she pinched his arm and leaned close to whisper hotly in his ear, "Stop it! You've no right! Keep your eyes to yourself!"

When he asked her, "What should I look at? I have to be looking at something," she told him, *sotto voce,* to imagine something in the middle of the air, anything; close his eyes if necessary, think about something else, pretend to be thinking if nothing came to him—it wasn't polite to stare!

Obedient, Bunce did as he was told; he thought about the cripple's short leg, imagined him lacing on the heavy shoe each morning, envisioned the clumping sound it made as the man walked, felt, in vague fashion, the cripple's embarrassment or pain.

Another time, with his father in a fine restaurant—Bunce was twelve—he saw a distinguished diner, a man with touches of theatrical grey at his temples, a man he'd overheard ordering wine with sophisticated authority, pick his nose while hiding behind his napkin, concealed from the scrutiny of all save Bunce. "Look!" he said behind his cupped hand to his father. "That guy looks like a zillionaire, he's got almost his whole finger shoved up his nose!"

"Mind your own beeswax!" his father said between clenched teeth. "What the hell's with you, you don't have any good manners? You trying to spoil my appetite with the prices they gouge here, kid?"

Bunce complied outwardly, but followed out of the corner of

his eye as the very distinguished diner withdrew his forefinger, examined its tip, wiped it on the underside of the upholstered chair, sipped his wine, patted his lips softly with his napkin, looked out over the restaurant with an expression of faintly contemptuous familiarity.

This, this sole individuating predeliction—a species of curiosity, an inexplicable fascination, a source of occasional satisfaction to him—stayed with Bunce throughout life. All his days, as an adolescent, pulling a two-year army stint as a draftee, in college, in married family life, on the job flogging insurance, Bunce watched.

A nondescript high schooler, more invisible than unpopular, Bunce descried the flaws in the seamless facades of those demi-gods and goddesses who reigned over the crowded halls, the athletic fields and gymnasium, the student council, social and special-interest clubs, such intellectual life as could be said to exist. He alone noted that Tammi Thompson, Prom Queen-elect, suffered a nagging skin problem, disguised the frequent eruptions marring her creamy cheeks and chin with skillfully blended pancake; it was Bunce who realized that Eddie Piotrowski, all-state wrestler and middle linebacker, was so nervous in classrooms his perspiration broke in huge rings plastering his sweatshirts to his muscled torso; only Bunce picked up on the fingernails, gnawed to the quick and beyond, of Jeffie Walker, lead-pipe cinch for valedictory laurels; it was Bunce who saw the run-down heels on the loafers of the snappiest dresser in the senior class, caught the plagiarized passage in a prize-winning essay, discovered the evidence of speech therapy in the barely controlled twitching lips of the lead actor in the Glee Club's annual drama.

Naturally, he shared nothing of any of this with anyone.

An E-3 assigned Quartermaster duty at one of the early remote missile silo locations in the Dakotas—he received the detachment's dirty linen each Wednesday morning, dispensed clean sheets that afternoon—Private First-Class Bunce observed his commanding officer was scarcely literate, so delivered all routine communications orally, struggled as if in combat when he read General Orders to his assembled ranks. Private First-Class Bunce, entering the latrine in the wee hours, stumbled by chance on his section sergeant practicing knotting his necktie before the mirror, never having learned the trick of it in his impoverished Oklahoma past. In the same latrine, seated on the commode, Private First-Class Bunce heard his outfit's two toughest customers—sluggers famed for their barroom brawls with townies—enter the next stall and engage, moaning with excitement, in an unnatural act clearly not their first mutual experience. The army was the loneliest period of Bunce's life.

A feckless student attending a mediocre land grant college in the Southwest, Bunce, out for a beer, came upon the English Department's sole scholar of any reputation in an out-of-the-way dive, so drunk he soiled his trousers while trying to recognize the door to the men's toilet; thereafter, at a well-attended lecture debunking New Criticism, Bunce focused on the professor's trembling hands, which rattled the manuscript he read from, the rosy flush and dry-mouthed pronunciation typical of the serious alcoholic. On a Coke date with the college dean's regular babysitter, Bunce, then a sophomore majoring in business administration, learned the dean had *not* resigned to enter the private sector as a corporate consultant. Such an airhead was this chatty co-ed, she did not realize the implications of her gossip—the dean, a man with a public persona much in demand as an inspirational speaker at Kiwanis, Rotary, and Chamber of Commerce banquets, had been given the boot by the regents for peculating endowment funds. Bunce, having chosen an isolated desk at the rear of the classroom, discerned that the clearest thinker enrolled in his Philosophy: Introduction to

Aesthetics course was, in the interims between his cogent, brilliantly articulated responses to the instructor's open queries, an inveterate player of pocket pool.

Bunce never spoke of these things to the girl he courted and made his wife in the middle of his junior year.

The ubiquitous intimacies afforded by marriage, steady employment, and fatherhood only exponentially increased the frequency of his perceptions. Never did Bunce *seek* these miniscule indices of the humanity of others—wife, daughter, colleagues, customers—no, they came upon him, thrust themselves against his sensibility, a rain, a blizzard of particulars revealing . . . nothing much, so far as Bunce ever thought about them.

Bunce found himself fixing on details: the black bristles his wife razored from her legs, flecking the bowl of their coral pink bathroom sink when he bent over it of a morning to perform his ablutions; the gum wrappers and popsicle sticks his daughter disposed of in his company car's ashtray, often jamming it open or shut; the back of the neck of his fellow agent, Paul Casey, periodically swathed in thick bandages that stank of ointment after electrolysis treatments for chronic acne; the peculiar attire of the nouveau riche contractor, one Paul Carter, to whom Bunce sold his first million-dollar term package—Carter wore rotting tennis shoes with his three-piece custom-tailored suit; the sharp intake of breath with which his wife, instead of a conventional *yes,* expressed assent or answered a casual query in the affirmative; the badly chipped front teeth of the Methodist clergyman who called on the Bunce household, to no avail, to cajole them into joining his congregation; the note to herself his teenage daughter wrote, then discarded in the kitchen's trash can reading: *when I get married I vow to have at least three kids minimum!!!!!! or else kill myself!!!!!!;* the cycles in which his district supervisor, one Dan Baker, grew long sideburns, goatees, and a moustache waxed in upturned horns, then shaved his face clean and had his hair cut in what they called a *fritz* in Bunce's high school days; the fact that his wife removed her shoes whenever seated in a public place, caressed the toes of one foot with those of the other; the one-armed mechanic, empty uniform sleeve neatly pinned just below the shoulder, who serviced Bunce's company car, who, whenever Bunce saw him in street clothes, wore an artificial arm with a white glove on its hand; the successful oil wildcatter to whom Bunce almost sold a million-dollar term package—the oilman carried several thousand dollars cash in a diamond-studded clip, but hated his given name, so he threw Bunce out of his office when he slipped and addressed him as *Oscar;* the way the melange of odors, both natural and artificial, his wife exuded permeated every common room in their house, while Bunce's seemed to have no tenacity at all; the fingers on the hands of the boy who took his daughter to her senior dance, each bearing a sloppily tattood letter, the aggregates spelling *love* and *hate;* the wear-soiled clip-on bow tie that Paul Casey wore every working day Bunce saw him, though he was otherwise well groomed; the permanent wrinkles in her forehead Bunce's wife developed over the years of their marriage from raising her brows unnaturally high whenever he spoke to her; that there appeared a thematic core, seen retrospectively, to his daughter's delight in, successively, her stroller, her scooter, her tricycle, her ten-speed, and the motorcycles owned by all her boyfriends; that Paul Casey and Dan Baker, though both avid fans of all professional sport, could not remember who won the World Series or Super Bowl only two or three years back; that his wife pronounced *etcetera* as *eck-cetera,* and refused to speak to him for a full twenty-four hours following the single occasion on which Bunce presumed to correct her; that Dan Baker kept an unopened pint of Ancient Age bourbon in his desk drawer, but, to Bunce's knowledge, did not drink except for beer while watching televised sports; that, when Paul Casey laughed, he actually, every time, said the words *hee hee!*; that, late in their marriage, whenever he proposed anything to his wife, she responded with *if you say so*; that the only customer Bunce ever knowingly screwed, selling him a policy certain to leave him insurance poor, had one ear apparently constructed of dark yellow wax or glossy rubber; that, when she informed him she wanted a divorce p.d.q., his wife, for the first time in years, did not lift her eyebrows as she listened to his futile effort to talk her out of it; that the first name of the biker who roared up on his Kawasaki to take Bunce's daughter away forever was Salvatore, the same as that of her two previous serious boyfriends; that, since Bunce had been abandoned by his wife and daughter, living alone, Paul Casey and Dan Baker fell silent whenever Bunce entered the office, but, soon after, came each in turn to tell him an outrageously obscene joke, slapped him on the back—Paul Casey laughed *hee hee!*, Baker a sort of gargled *haw haw!*; that most people fell into one of two categories, those who said *one*, as in *one has to consider the options*, those who said *we*, as in *we don't want to rush into anything* . . .

Thus was Bunce's life, the essence of the quotidian save for this unending, unsought, unexamined storm of palpable detail, signifying—for all Bunce knew or cared—absolutely nothing. Zip. Zed. Zilch.

Until he moved into his tract house on the cul-de-sac in Nottingham Estates, and, outside the now effortless-as-living-itself routines by which he hawked his insurance wares, Bunce began to think about it. At which juncture, by virtue of no more than sheer proximity and a total dearth of distraction, he developed a steadily growing interest in his neighbors.

Initially, Bunce was as indifferent to his new neighbors as they were toward him. The first week in his new house on the cul-de-sac, he feared the sort of scripted gesture of welcome his ex-wife never failed to extend when she saw a moving van deliver a new family's possessions to their block: a platter of store-bought chocolate chip cookies or gummy home-baked cake, a tasteless casserole. But he was spared this perfunctory hospitality and was grateful. The inhabitants of the homes that flanked his, two on each side, remained the fleetingly glimpsed figures who spoke, when it could not be avoided, as laconically as Bunce himself.

To Bunce's left, on the southern tip of the paved arc they shared, lived a family named The Kintners, Grubgeld told him. "He's in my racket, but he's *big*! Runs his own agency, in tight with the banks hereabouts, he don't sweat qualifying *his* people for mortgages!" The Kintners, Bunce observed, exhibited a sort of shining symmetry: father, mother, teenage son, daughter about ten or eleven. They might have stepped from a page in *Family Living* or *Suburban Dweller*. The son—Bunce overheard him called *Junior*—was a three-fourths-scale clone of his father, both of them dark-haired, deeply and evenly tanned, robust with energy, even possessing the same exaggerated gait, a springy stride suggesting enthusiasm, confidence, a serenity bordering on bliss. The daughter—Missy, Bunce heard them address her—might have been modeled on her mother by the same artisan so pleased with the original he duplicated her, half-size, in the child. They were towhead blondes, petite almost to the point of looking anorexic, walked each with the hesitant, mincing step Bunce associated with bound feet; when they smiled—without speaking—at Bunce as they chanced on occasion to pass, they pulled back their red lips to expose gleaming, feral teeth. Bunce never got close enough to be sure Missy wore the same cosmetics her mother did.

As a family, their most striking characteristic was their sumptuary elegance and grooming; Bunce had never seen people

who owned so many clothes, so many color-coordinated outfits. His finances severely depleted by divorce and closing costs,
Bunce shuddered to imagine their dry-cleaning bills, the bucks
they must have laid out regularly on hairdressers and stylists to
maintain their coiffures.

Sandwiched between Bunce and Max Kintner's super-whole-
some brood lived a nun, Sister Mary Angelica Hanrahan, an
uncloistered Benedictine. "You can't tell by looking," Grubgeld
told Bunce, "she traipses around in dungarees and T-shirts and
what-not-all. Maybe you read about her in the paper? She's
supposedly some kind of social worker missionary, what she's
really is a monster pain in the keester, pops off at city council
meetings about E.R.A. and women's lib and all. Hey," he said to
Bunce, "ix-nay on mentioning the otective-pray ause-clay, that
ovenant-cay, where she can hear you, she'd take me to the
Supreme Court or set up a halfway house here for spite to
knock the bottom out of the property values. I mean," Grubgeld
said, "this old bitch is what we called in the service Section 8,
get my drift?"

Sister Mary Angelica Hanrahan did affect stone-washed blue
jeans and sweatshirts with the sleeves chopped raggedly off at
the shoulders, sandals that revealed her bony, lilac-tinged big
feet and horny toes. She was, Bunce agreed with Grubgeld's
verdict when he finally glimpsed her, a long string of spit,
mannish, coming and going from the cul-de-sac in a rustbody
stationwagon—the antithesis of the Kintner's simonized sedan
—with a punctured muffler, its dented bumpers adorned with
glow-in-the-dark stickers that said *Save The Whales, Nobody
Wins Nuclear War, Nicaragua = Vietnam?, God Loves You—Pray
To Her, ERA Now!*.

On his right resided another unattached female, Megan Mc-
Clard, reputed to be a poetess. "Which is to say," said Grubgeld
with a wink so emphatic it nearly closed both his eyes, "a guy

with the right line could, if you get me, arrange it on the side sort of for emergencies in the case you're struck out elsewhere, if I'm making myself clear? Which is to say," he added, "there's no wild parties or any such'll disturb you. I'm just going by the looks of her. For all I know she could be AC-DC, plus also the general idea of divorcées, including some personal experiences I won't rehash you since we're here on business, right?"

Megan McClard did display a choreographed Bohemianism. By contrast with the Kintners' manicured lawn, thriving shrubbery, and newly painted trim, her home was a shambles; her grass was grown to hay, hedges blighted, windows draped with what looked like bedsheets, one broken pane patched with a square of plywood; her mode of attire greatly exceeded the uncloistered nun's in its deliberate slovenliness—she wore military surplus uniforms and a pair of boots Bunce recognized as the match of his daughter's biker paramour's. Her hair was cut shorter than Dan Baker's in his *fritz* cycle, reminding Bunce of an old *Life* photo of a French collaborator after her punishment for cohabiting with Nazis. She arrived and departed with her hands thrust in her fatiques' cargo pockets, books and thick sheafs of manuscript tucked under one arm. "I figure she's on alimony, no other visible means of support. I mean," Grubgeld said, "what could she do for a living, work in a car wash?"

At the north end of the cul-de-sac was the house of Professor Wendell Mayo. Said Grubgeld, "Somebody told me he's a big intellectual mucky-muck at the A&M College. You probably won't lay eyes on him once in a blue moon, he's probably thinking intellectual thoughts or studying crap to teach his classes in whatever."

It was many days before Bunce encountered Professor Mayo, and he looked as Bunce thought a professor should, distracted, tardy, veiled from the superficial surface of reality by the inner fog of cogitation in which he elected to exist. He wore plain suits shiny with wear, ties that did not go with his dull browns and blues, a bulging briefcase with a broken latch, had a wife and three daughters who seemed equally oblivious of him, donned floppy galoshes at the slightest hint of damp weather, swathed himself in a scarf if a breeze arose, passed by Bunce as though his neighbor was invisible. He commuted to the A&M College on an old girl's bicycle.

"This house has your name on it," Grubgeld assured Bunce, uttering his clincher. "You'll fit in like a bandit! I double damn guaran-damn-tee you!"

And he did.

Bunce's early scrutiny of his neighbors was casual, wholly unintentional. Leaving for work early one Thursday, he chanced to look at the trash set out at the curb in front of Professor Wendell Mayo's house for the municipal garbage pickup. His eye was caught by the glint of the morning sun reflected off the contents of a huge cardboard packing case. Slowing as he passed it in his car, he found it was a mounded heap of empty longnecker beer bottles, a brand he knew was the cheapest available.

The evening paper carried a terse report of the monthly open meeting of the city council; Sister Mary Angelica Hanrahan had dominated and extended the proceedings with an appeal that became an harangue: she requested, then demanded, an ordinance mandating the deletion of the sexist generic *he* from all written documents generated at taxpayers' expense, and its obligatory replacement with the egalitarian *s/he*. The council, unwilling to act on the instant, tabled the request for further study; Sister Hanrahan lambasted the councilpersons in the letters-to-the-editor column of the following evening's edition, signing herself *Ms. M. A. Hanrahan, Citizen-Activist.*

Bunce spent much of one Sunday afternoon behind the curtain on his living room's picture window, watching the Kintner family working with the coordinated efficiency of a hive of bees, washing and waxing the family sedan in their driveway. Father Max wielded the hose; mother vacuumed and wiped down the interior, cleaned the windows inside; son swabbed with a sponge, dried off the chrome in tandem with his father, each armed with a floppy chamois; the little girl knelt gracefully to scour the whitewalls with a toothbrush. They labored with an intensity that rendered them oblivious to the sparkling day around them, had no need to communicate as they strove, as if each's role in this division of effort had been preassigned, practiced, the performance of their respective tasks a drill of military precision.

Bunce watched, fascinated as much by their apparel—father, mother, son, daughter, all wore the same appropriate uniform: laundry-fresh plaid shirt, tail hanging out, sleeves rolled neatly back to the elbows, pressed jeans, clean running shoes. Though it was a breezy day, their sprayed hair never fluttered. Bunce, held fast at his post behind the curtain, watched throughout, from the moment they came out of their house in a phalanx, hose, buckets, sponges, chamois, and Windex in hand like weapons, to the end, when they gathered it all and disappeared inside in formation. Bunce's final vision was the sedan gleaming like a showroom model in the overhead sun that quickly dried the water from the drive's spotless pavement.

Late, past midnight, unable to sleep, Bunce got up, dressed, went for a stroll through Nottingham Estates. Returning to his cul-de-sac after an hour's brisk walk that failed to dissipate the nagging consciousness of something he could not define, he paused under the stars before Megan McClard's house. He looked up at the black dome of the sky that covered him, picked out with twinkling points, held his breath for a moment, heard a faint singing.

Bunce did not at first recognize the tune, struck with the

pristine purity of the voice rendering it, its quality a crystalline brilliance of earnest innocence. It came to his ears, he realized, from within the poetess's unlit house—she had to be singing, sending up her wonderful music to be lost in empty blackness! Then he marked the song; it was "Because"; it had been sung to an organ accompaniment in the campus chapel where he was married. Bunce stood, listened, wondered at the Bohemian literati's singing to no one save herself in the dark of her neglected domicile, remembered the thrill of tenderness and confident aspiration he felt on his long-past wedding day, and realized, when Megan McClard's ethereal soprano ceased without a flaw, that whatever troubled him, prevented the sleep he so needed against the day to come, had evaporated with her last ringing note. He could not remember sleeping so soundly in years.

He had no reason to expect Grubgeld to telephone. "It's me. Grubgeld," Grubgeld said. "The guy sold you the house, I'm checking to see if you still love me like you did the day we closed? What, you forgot me already?"

"Of course not. I just didn't recognize your voice at first."

"I'm like that," the real estate salesman said, "I got a face nobody recalls or something. I must not make an impression. Whereas I make it a point of priding myself on never forgetting anybody. Which is why I'm calling, I like to follow up and see my people are satisfied, it's professional with me."

"I was just surprised to hear from you again. It's unusual," Bunce said.

"Yeah," Grubgeld said. "So," he said, "you happy with the dream house I fixed you up with?"

"It's fine. I'm fine," Bunce said.

"Yeah. Right. Good. What I like to hear," he said, "my people satisfied with the job I do them." When Bunce could think of nothing to say, did not speak, Grubgeld said, "So, how's life treating you? Getting any?"

"Any what?"

"Give me a break, Bunce," Grubgeld said, "it's quiet ones like you have to beat it off with a stick. Me, I chase gash seven nights a week, you could count my action on your two thumbs."

"Oh," said Bunce. "Yeah. I mean I get your meaning. No, I'm just getting through it day by day. I lead a very peaceful existence," he said.

"Sure," Grubgeld said, "don't tell me. A true gentleman doesn't talk, right? Anyhow. Your neighbors not intruding?"

"They're fine. I hardly know they're there."

"You read where your whacko libber nun made the paper again?" he asked.

"I read that. I never see her, she must be out and around a lot."

"Minding other people's business," Grubgeld said. "Anyway," he said, "just calling to check back if you're happy in the house. And let you know, give me a ring any problems come up, plumbing clogs or the roof caves in, whatever."

"I appreciate that," Bunce said.

"Yeah. Right." After another silence, Bunce scrambling to think of a polite way to get off the phone, Grubgeld said, "Say. It's still early hours. You feel like coming out to join me, what say we tip a few, see if we can glom on a couple of strays?"

"No," Bunce said. "I mean, I'm bushed, rough day, tomorrow's a toughie."

After another silence, Grubgeld said, "Yeah. Right. Okay. Well. So, give me a hoot on the horn if I can help any way, huh?"

"Yeah," Bunce said. "Right."

It was the sheer bone-deep boredom of his plodding life-style that led Bunce to take the step from passive observation to active inquiry into the lives of his neighbors on the cul-de-sac. His days given over to the mechanical pursuit of dollars that came to him in an adequate flow, the quest too familiar to offer the excitement of challenge, his nights a desert of routines—the six o'clock news on the tube, bland suppers, the daily newspaper's timeless trivia, long walks through the streets of Nottingham Estates to tire him sufficiently to permit sleep—where else was there for Bunce to turn for sanity's diversion except the four households in such immediate proximity?

Having written off his wife and daughter, treated in the office by Paul Casey and Dan Baker like a species of emotional leper whose recent infection might be contagious, the only fellow human he even considered calling was Grubgeld, a prospect that literally made Bunce sweat and shiver.

So Bunce turned, though with little sense of significance, to the Kintner family, Professor Wendell Mayo, Megan McClard, and Sister Mary Angelica Hanrahan, O.B.E. The initiation of dossiers on each felt logical, an insurance man's habit of giving substance to information and speculation that might otherwise have assumed no coherent shape. His customary nocturnal perambulations offered a convenient mode.

Professor Wendell Mayo was the simplest. Bunce checked the renowned academic's trash, set out for municipal pickup each Sunday and Wednesday evening. In the file, legal pad sheets stored in a manila folder, Bunce wrote: —*it is impossible to make an exact count of the longnecker beer bottles Prof. M. throws away twice a week—my best guess is the man is going through about half a case per diem to produce the piles he sets out?—the possibility he only drinks half that, his wife chugs her fair share?—is such drinking done on steady basis during day or binge late at night after his work is done?—notes: make a point of checking out appearance in early AM see if he looks hung over— approach house for closer look?—*

Bunce's Neighbors

Coming back to his house after an especially long walk begun very late at night, seeing no evidence of light, no sign of wakeful occupants in any of his neighbors' dwellings, Bunce was hit with a sudden inspiration to open Megan McClard's mailbox—standing, like all those on the cul-de-sac, like a curbside sentinel awaiting relief from the postman—and examine the contents thereof: outgoing mail. In her file, Bunce wrote: *are all poets this prolific?—what sort of poems do they print in magazines like SatEvePost, Bride, Good Housekeeping, Cosmo?—note: check public lib to see if she has ever published a book?—do all poetesses send their work in scented envelopes?—check at post office to see when Emily Dickinson stamps were issued—still available or purchased in bulk?—pretentious to identify self as poet in return address?—or just honest?—worth risking fed offense conviction to swipe one for reading?—better: take one, steam open, reseal and drop in mailbox the next day?—*

His first glimpse behind the seamless facade projected by Max Kintner and his family was a stroke of dumb luck; someone—the son?—forgot to close the garage door. Bunce, enjoying the tingle of apprehension that tickled his stomach, echoed in his toes and the tips of his fingers, scurried up their driveway for a quick perusal of what was revealed in the full moon's light. In the file, labeled *Kintner Menage*, Bunce wrote: *Chaos!—how the hell do they find anything when they need it?!?!—garage interior so crowded with junk barely room for automobile!—packrat impulse causing saving of old newspapers in stacks falling over?—boxes of canning jars, hand-tools, coils of wire, old bike innertubes, scraps of lumber, old rug rolled and stuck up in rafters, spider webs, mouse droppings on oil-stained paint-spattered floor—all coated with thick dust-dirt like abandoned city dump they forgot to bulldoze over!—could living space within house even slightly resemble?!?!?!?*

Bunce's first entry in Sister Mary Angelica Hanrahan's dossier required the first excruciatingly deliberate effort on his part. On a cloudy night when even the full moon was obscured, he darted across the swath of grass separating his house from hers, drawn by a flickering will o' the wisp light behind the curtain of what he was sure was a bedroom window. He paused, crouched a moment in the black corner where her privacy fence joined the wall, waited to be sure the street out front was clear, then tiptoed close, placed his ear flush against the cold pane. Cheek chilled by the glass, he stopped his breath to listen.

Bunce wrote: *stake my life it was Latin!—Gregorian chanting?—a recorded accompaniment, organ, to Sr. A.'s voice?—punctuated by sobbing/whimpering?—religious ecstasy? (more like listening to sex!)—if standard R. C. practice, why lateness of hour?—check out a Sunday, see if Sr. A. attends local parish observance?—question: is prying into area of religion going too far? (maybe, but does this qualify as relig?)—strobelike illumination behind curtain from numerous and large candles?—*

Bunce was rereading his notes when Grubgeld telephoned the second time. "It's me. Grubgeld. Grubgeld?" he said.

"Oh. Right. I thought I recognized your voice this time," Bunce said.

"That's at least encouraging," Grubgeld said. "Well. Hey. Listen, I just called on the spur of the moment here."

"The house's fine. I'm really truly satisfied with the deal we made," Bunce said.

"No," the real estate salesman said. "I'm not calling in my professional role, I mean. I got this new membership to a private club I heard about, sort of a key club, and I can bring a guest, I thought I'd ask you if you felt like going. They say you can't turn around without bumping into really prime stuff just begging to give it away free, they say the broads outnumber the guys two, three to one! Interested?"

"No," Bunce said. "Thanks for asking me, I'm not up for that yet these days."

"Post-traumatic depression," Grubgeld said, "I went through it both times we split the blanket, hell, I go through it every time I blow a relationship with a woman! The only cure's get out and get some stinky on your dinky, Bunce, take it from an expert."

"I don't think so. Really, though, thanks for asking."

"Oh," Grubgeld said. "Okay. Sure. Well, I understand. I remember the pain. Maybe next time, except right now they got this special discount on new memberships, you could miss out if you sit around suffering too long."

"Maybe," Bunce said, relieved when Grubgeld said he'd touch base back with him in a while, then hung up.

Bunce took a clean sheet of yellow legal pad paper, wrote: *start a file on Grubgeld?—no (lives too far away to get involved with)—*

Staying on the alert yielded no new intelligence of his neighbors. Professor Wendell Mayo's outflow of longnecker empties continued. The Max Kintner family revealed no gap in the flawless facade of their collective grooming. An afternoon's library research turned up no literary journals, however obscure or fugitive, containing poems by Megan McClard. Sister Mary Angelica Hanrahan made the newspaper again, this time with an open letter calling on the city's oppressed underclass—anyone of what she called *dark complected peoples and those preferring minority sexual practices*—to join with women everywhere in the coming world struggle to throw off the joke of white male domination.

So Bunce's file grew, but only a little; it read redundantly to him; he had, he realized, discovered the stuff of mystery, and must now solve it. More concerted efforts were called for. And God and Bunce knew there was nothing else in his life worthy of his attention.

Bunce dressed himself ninja-style—black shoes and socks, dark blue slacks, a black turtleneck sweater, a navy wool cap—the better to cloak himself in the night, but stopped short of smearing his face with burnt cork. Well past midnight, he dashed furtively across his lawn, past Megan McClard's deteriorating house, from which came the beatific singing she did several nights a week—Bunce heard "I Love You Truly" this time—to Professor Mayo's.

Luck was with Bunce; it was far easier than he anticipated, a wide gap in the drapery drawn over the window of the scholar's den-study provided him a panoramic view. Bunce, his heart thudding in his chest, breath uneven, mouth dry as paper, was able to see the whole of the room, fix the vision in his mind's eye for recapitulation in the copious notes he entered, as dawn broke over Nottingham Estates, in the professor's file.

Bunce wrote: *Prof. Mayo is a fraud!—where expect to find an intellectual in private moments: reading books? preparing lectures? composing an article? playing chess? engaged in pure contemplation of the aesthetic, eternal, infinite? No way! Prof. M. revealed as man with soul of proletarian!*

—setting appropriate—den-study (floor plans identical in all N. Estates houses?) walls lined with built-in shelves, solid rows of books (too far away to make out titles—check out with binoculars next time?)—read once if at all? Ever reread? Briefcase on floor beside relaxalounger chair (still buckled shut!)—clarity of vision dim in haze of cigar smoke hanging in layers, same from stogie held in teeth—on side of lounger opposite briefcase sits case of longneckers (⅓ consumed—empties tossed on carpet (wife picks up to set out for trash pickup?)—bottle caps strewn about—opener in easy reach beside ashtray on chairside table filled with dead

chewed wet-end stogie butts, magazines (unable to make out titles: Playboy? Hustler?)—obvious center focal point of room is big-screen TV, primary light source, tuned to Australian rules football game! (remote control channel changer resting on M's bloated belly, but stays with match throughout duration observed—watched commercials with equal attention!)—

Prof. M. stretched out almost full length on lounger, remote control rising/falling with breathing (falls off when coughing on cigar), holds in place with free hand while swigging longnecker (downed three during period observed, chug-a-lug style with last!)—Prof. wears filthy sweatshirt, grey (dirty-white?) wash pants, bare feet (dirty!)—overall impression: totally absorbed in mindless violence of Australian rules football, swigging long-neckers reflex action (natural as breath!), occasional vigorous scratching of scalp, armpit, groin region—lifts hips when expelling gas?—

Conclusions: Prof. Wendell Mayo is absolute mirror opposite of public appearance/role! Briefcase is pure prop! Exhibits in private true essence of sensual self-indulgent slob!

Queries: how able to get by in A&M college context role of intellectual/teacher-molder of young? how achieved reputed rep as scholarly expert?—is truth revealed above result of decline from early-life idealism/ambitions? Or: truth revealed there from start, skill at concealing actuality identity from students, peer colleagues, academic administrative superiors?—

Who would believe if told? Document? Tell who??? To what purpose?!?!?—

Although he did not sleep at all that night, Bunce suffered no weariness through the following day's work; oblivious to the awkward demeanors Paul Casey and Dan Baker affected in his presence, he thought only of the coming night, the excursion he would make across Sister Mary Angelica Hanrahan's lawn to the Max Kintner household. He was unprepared when Casey and Baker came to his desk in tandem, solemn expressions adorning their faces, and spoke directly to him for the first time since his divorce.

"How you doing, really, Bunce?" Paul Casey asked.

"I'm fine," he said.

"You seem kind of different today all of a sudden," Dan Baker said, "your ex or your kid giving you any special grief or anything?"

"No," Bunce said. "Not at all. Far from it. They're completely out of touch, so what could they do to upset me? No, really, I appreciate your asking," he said, "but I'm fine. Never felt better."

His excitement, the secret inner joy sparked by this new, unsought passion in his life, Bunce thought, must show! He resolved to hide it better, ploughed into his work with an intensity and a determination that only increased as the day wore away toward his planned rendezvous with the Kintner household.

But, that night, just as he was about to go out, garbed in his ninja costume, Grubgeld telephoned.

"Bunce," the real estate salesman said, "it's me, Grubgeld. You recognize my voice, Bunce?"

"Of course," Bunce said. "Where are you? You sound funny, Grubgeld."

"I should," Grubgeld said, "I'm drunk on my ass. I'm using the phone the bartender so kindly allowed me to call a cab to take home 'cause I'm too fried to operate a motor vehicle, but instead I decided to call my old pal Bunce. How you doing, Bunce?"

"You're for sure drunk," Bunce said. "You better get that cab and get some sleep, Grubgeld, you're going to be hurting if you have to get up and work early tomorrow."

"Who shivs a git?" the real estate salesman said. "Do you know you're the only person in the world I got to talk to, Bunce? I was talking with a female here earlier, but I probably said something gross, on account of she ditched me. Bitch said she was going to the can, the next time I looked for her she was dust. Now my bartender friend here won't talk to me anymore, Bunce, so what's a person supposed to do, curl up and die? Talk to me, Bunce!" Grubgeld said.

"What do you want me to say?" Bunce asked, then stood, dressed like an Oriental assassin in the kitchen of his house on the cul-de-sac street in Nottingham Estates, while Grubgeld talked and talked about how a person had to have someone to talk to to keep sane, to keep from feeling like hanging himself, to keep from feeling like the world didn't shiv a git for him if he lived or not. Grubgeld was interrupted by the bartender often, and there were long pauses, and for a while it sounded like the real estate salesman was weeping.

The only time Bunce got a chance to get a word in, he asked him, "Grubgeld, what do you know about Mayo, the professor lives down on the corner? Can you tell me anything about him? Do you know very much about him, or the poet or the nun, the guy Kintner you say is such a hotshot in real estate? Grubgeld?" But the bartender had apparently taken the phone away from Grubgeld; Bunce received no answers. And when he checked his watch, it was too late to go out to observe the Kintner family, and Bunce was suddenly tired.

He napped for a few hours, woke just as false dawn came to the sky over Nottingham Estates, and, to avoid a total loss, went outside in the hope his clothes would pass for jogger's togs, which is how he came to see Max Kintner and his family in the performance of their morning's ablutions.

Bunce wrote: —*Confusion! Disarray! Chaos!—a rat's nest of carelessness, slovenly neglect!—their preparation a studied panic, Chinese fire drill,—a wonder, a miracle they manage so well!— how do they make it to work/school on time?*

(observation risky as hell: avoid in future except in dark!—

*running from window to window exhausting!—fragmented glimpses
of revealed truth like disorder perceived!)—*

Consider:

*—household interior is mirror-image of garage mess previously
noted: 3 locations (master bedroom, living room, bath) almost
indistinguishable by virtue of clothing lying about ubiquitous—
K. family moves as group from one to the next, obvious customary* AM
*procedure to produce selves for day they face to come—how find
coordinated items of attire in such hopeless jumble!?!?*

*—master bedroom: father Max and spouse rip at suits/dresses in
walk-in closet, heaving discards to floor, wire hangers clattering,
donning (then doffing after self-scrutiny in full-length mirror) series of outfits take turns appraising the other's appearance—strike
poses like runway models, store dummies—sounds of debate/
argument over suitability of given dress/suit—throughout which
son and little girl appear, disappear, reappear (from respective bedrooms?) in succession of outfits, pose for parents, arguments/debates
result in children's tears!—all but little girl eventually satisfied
(shared communal smiles, father/mother/son parade elected dress),
move to living room to complete her apparel—(very risky move to
front of house to observe; luck of sliver of space at edge of picture
window—observation under duress ref. concern for passing motor-
ist pedestrian exposing activity!)—*

*—living room: little girl near hysterics, father/mother/bro select
skirts, blouses, vests, blazers, sweaters, stockings from among
items lying about on furniture, on carpet—hold up for inspection/
appraisal (rejection by head-shaking, some tried on, rejected with
foot stomping!)—culminates in reluctant approval/acceptance of
school-girl middie outfit—family walks (in celebration?) in stately
circle in room, exchange smiles, cut glances at large wall mirror
over sofa, gather for embrace—to bathroom!*

(great relief at position outside b.r. shielded from street!—sun

*coming up!—blinds tilted just enough to allow full view—unable
to hear conversation due to whine of hair dryers)—*

*—bathroom: considerable skill and coord. of prep. of coiffures!
—rotation over sink to wash hair (one shampooing, one blow-
drying, one combing out, one applying scent-tonic!)—rapid lather,
rinse, blow-dry styling and comb-out—huddled to see selves as
group, skin glistening with colognes, in wall-length mirror—
beaming approval, lips move in obvious reciprocity of congrats!—
final result suitable for framing!*

*(depart in haste at sound of trash pickup at work at Prof M's
house—crash of longnecker empties in dumpster!—home to write
this, get ready for office)—*

*Query: if we could see ourselves as others see us? Any positive
effect? Worth the trouble? (think about these things!)—*

"How," Bunce asked Dan Baker at the office that day, "do you
decide what to wear for the day when you get up in the morning, Dan?"

"What?" Dan said. "What kind of a dopey thing is that to ask
a man? If you really want to know, I don't. The wife decides for
me. By the time I'm done with my annual morning dump she's
got it all laid out for me on the bed. I get dressed and eat and
then head out. Why'd you ask, Bunce?"

"Just curious," Bunce said. "How come you keep changing
from having a beard to shaving it off clean?"

"You need to get a interest in your life, I'd say," his boss said.

"I got a system," Paul Casey said when Bunce put the ques-
tion to him. "You never noticed, did you. I got exactly six suits.
One for each day. Sundays I slob it. Monday I wear Monday's,
Tuesday, and so on. Plus I always wear the same tie."

"I never noticed," Bunce said.

"Probably," Paul Casey said, "because every month or so I

switch the days around. Then, like, my Monday suit's my Thursday or my Saturday, like that. Who wants to know?"

"Just curious," Bunce told him. Paul Casey and Dan Baker stayed away from him that day, and Bunce caught them staring at him, whispering, but did not mind.

Bunce's chest and stomach fluttered, a giddiness seized his brain, when he thought of the risk he had taken in the day's first light to watch the Kintner family, so he resolved to check out the poetess and the nun only under cover of night. There were several futile efforts before he succeeded with Megan McClard, scaling her privacy fence, locating a shade lifted just enough to permit his view of the hall leading from her bedroom to the den-study, where, he could only speculate, she underwent some sort of solitary ceremony following upon the slow processional to music he watched through the window from her backyard, a lonely dog yowling somewhere in the distance.

In her file, Bunce, shaken, after staring at the blank yellow legal pad, recorded: *Oh sad! Sad! Sad!—oh how very very very sad!—*

Query: why do they hide themselves? why mask truths? does anyone/everyone guess at the possibilities? if so, why do we lie to ourselves?!?!?

—where to begin?—

—ethereal, virginal, romantic—did my wife look this way at our wedding?—

—M. McClard (dresses in bedroom?) emerges into corridor preceded by organ music ("Here Comes the Bride"—hi-fi on loud from bedroom, distinct from where I stand at backyard window!) —the most elaborate wedding dress I ever saw (family heirloom?)—M. M. halfway down corridor to den-study before end of train appears from b.r. doorway—her pace of progress is solemn perfection timed to music—in place of bouquet, carries fat sheaf of papers (poetry manuscripts!), dropping along route like flower

girl scattering rose petals!—her face barely visible (eyes lowered) beneath embroidered lace veil—full ten min. to reach den-study, train following—organ continues, then silence (empty hall with scattered poems on carpet)—

—possible to image ceremony M. M. performs alone in den-study (read aloud wedding/marriage/love poems?)—no way to see in!—shutters fast—unable to hear even with ear at window!—

—monstrous!—sick!—

—holy—

—unable to decide on tears or laughter correct reaction!

oh sadness!

oh frail, damaged, suffering young poetess!

Oh the Humanity!

Query: ask self, why are you doing this!?!? Are you as sick as she? Bunce, is it wise to know what others would never confess to? Dare tell what you know to others? Casey? Baker? Is it healthy to think of these things, Bunce?

Conclusion: oh what a thing to see, to think, to know what fellow humankind can be!!!!

Query: better to know, or only guess, or completely ignore truth (Truth!)? What is Truth? Is knowledge power or doom? Ignorance bliss? Quit now? Live and let live? Live and learn? How to live! Dare to live????

—Sad—

Bunce had not decided to continue his activity when Grubgeld telephoned again. "Mr. Bunce?" the real estate salesman said, "this is Grubgeld. Can we possibly talk for a second?"

"Hello, Grubgeld," Bunce said. "I recognize your voice."

"Right," Grubgeld said. "I guess you would by now. Which is why I'm calling you. If you've got a spare minute to talk, I mean."

"I've got nothing pressing to do," he told him.

"Yeah. Well. I'm calling to apologize for my call the other

night there. I guess I was so schnockered in my cups I got a little crazy. It only came back to me when I sobered up how I rang you up and bent your ear there all bent out of shape, I wanted you to know I'm ashamed and sorry for it."

"It's okay," Bunce said. "We all do odd things now and again, Grubgeld."

"No," the real estate salesman said. "I mean, it's not the sort of person I am. I mean, I'm not the world's best person or the smartest, I've had some lumps in my time, two bad marriages and I tip the glass too much sometimes and all, but I consider myself a very professional businesslike man. I work at my job, a lot depends on making a good impression in the sales profession, so I feel really crappy harassing you a client of mine especially when I should know better than to be out bar hopping like some wild man."

"Forget it," Bunce said, "it's forgotten."

"Good," Grubgeld said. "I mean, thanks. And I promise you you won't get any more whacko calls from me in the middle of the night, okay?"

"Okay," Bunce said, "feel free to phone me if you want, I understand," he said.

"You mean that?" Grubgeld said.

"I think I do," Bunce said, and when he hung up, he had decided to learn such truth as he could about Sister Mary Angelica Hanrahan.

When he had done so, had stood for half an hour outside her window dressed in his ninja costume, looking and listening, Bunce found himself unable to write anything in the liberated activist nun's file.

"Did you study Latin in school?" Bunce asked Paul Casey at the office.

"Are you kidding, Bunce? I was strictly a screw-off as a student. Why?" he asked.

"I did. They made us at parochial school," Dan Baker said.

"*Mea culpa* means, like, I'm guilty, is that right?" Bunce said.

"Yeah. At least I think so. Why?" Dan Baker said.

"I just wondered," Bunce said. Then he asked them both, "Do you believe in God? I mean a God who punishes people for their sins? Do you guys believe we're all sinners?" Bunce asked. "Do you think we have to punish ourselves for what we do that we think's wrong or sinful, even if possibly nobody else knows we did it or we're not even sure what we did was wrong or a sin?" he asked them.

There was a silence between them, and Paul Casey and Dan Baker looked at each other, then at Bunce before they spoke. "Hey, Bunce," Paul Casey said, "that's pretty off the wall, man!"

"Bunce," Dan Baker said, "do you maybe need some time off, buddy? I'm sort of wondering if you should get some counseling or talk to somebody you trust, I don't like what I'm hearing here, Bunce."

"Maybe," Bunce said, "you're right, I don't know." When he repeated his questions, insisted they answer, Paul Casey said he never thought about God, he figured life was all fate; Dan Baker said he still believed what he had been taught in parochial school, but could not remember much of it.

Bunce wrote: —*no need to research Latin beyond mea culpa, says it all!—oh, Sister Hanrahan, what do you think you have done to require this!—a tradition of self-flagellation in her church to account for it?—dear Sister A., doesn't the world mock you enough to pay for your transgressions?—thinks God mocks her in similar fashion, degree?—*

Query: how often must she beat self with that whip (welts, skin broken!)? Gets medical treatment after such?—relig. purpose signified in candles on table-altar, kneeling posture (awkward to flail backside over shoulder!)—

—needs self-abuse to cover public notoriety/scorn via news-

paper reports of social agitation, obvious indifference of populace to causes she touts?—

What does she say in confessional?!?!

—seeking sainthood?—

Bunce, taking some solace from the fact that he had looked away when the nun turned toward the window, exposing her blue-veined, shriveled breasts, wrote: *Oh God! Oh Man! Oh Woman! Professor! Max! Megan! Angelica! Bunce,* he wrote, *is there nothing you can do to help?!?!?!?*

And then Bunce could write no longer, and it was a day and a night, and yet another day, early in the evening, when he knew his neighbors on the cul-de-sac street were all at home, before Bunce was able to answer his own question.

There was a glorious sunset behind Bunce as he stood in the middle of the street, facing the truncated arc of tract houses; the light bathed his house, the houses of his neighbors, in a red-gold glow, and Bunce, his manila dossiers clutched to his chest like armor, drew himself up to his full height to address them as though he held the stage of an open-air amphitheater. He stood there, waited a bit, both to firm his resolve and to allow time for the others to arrive; they would come any moment now. Bunce was confident they were coming.

"This isn't a really good time for me, Mr. Bunce," Grubgeld said when Bunce phoned to invite him. "I really appreciate your asking me over, especially after the stunt I pulled calling you like I did, but I usually hit this one place has a two-for-one happy hour about now, there's this certain gal hangs out there I'm trying to hit on if you get my intention. You really want me to drop over, it's that important to you?" the real estate sales-man said. Bunce knew he would come.

And Paul Casey and Dan Baker would come, Bunce was certain. "Is this business, Bunce?" Dan asked.

Bunce's Neighbors

"You'll have to forgive me," Paul said, "seeing as how this is pretty much a surprise out of the blue, you calling me up to visit you at your place, Bunce." They would come, if only because they believed he needed looking after, had freaked out at last, their suspicions confirmed; Bunce knew they would arrive any moment now.

He wanted them all out there in the cul-de-sac street with him, together. Bunce clutched his files, looked at his neighbors' houses, pulsing with the red-gold of the sunset as if the private truths of their inhabitants ticked and beat with an intensity threatening to burst free of the facades concealing them from the eyes of the world.

Bunce was too far out in the empty street to hear anything, but he imagined the scenes within as clearly as though the houses were built with walls of glass. To his right, he imagined the Max Kintner household in a confused flurry of motion, seeking and selecting the appropriate evening mode of attire, crowding the messy bathroom to check their hair, dab on fresh scents, inspect and admire one another in their house's many mirrors; next door, he conceived Sister Mary Angelica Hanrahan, perhaps even now stripping herself, lighting candles, reaching for the scourge, muttering in ecclesiastical Latin; to his left, behind the unkempt Bohemian exterior, might not the poetess, Megan McClard, be this instant arraying herself as a bride of pristine innocence, choosing organ music, gathering her new poems, her love letters to the spectral groom she wed in ceremonies of her own creation? And next door to her, the dinner hour past, surely Professor Wendell Mayo had already ensconced himself before his big-screen television to puff rank stogies, swill beer from longnecker bottles, scratch and fart and escape the lie of his intellectuality in the mindless throes of violent sport or cheap melodrama!

Oh! Bunce thought, *the humanity!*

And Bunce looked at his own tract house, so red with the peak of the sunset at his back it looked as if it burned with the secret truth of his life: he had, in the past two and a half days' unceasing introspection, discovered—that behind and beneath the supremely dull, mundane persona he had lived with and as all the prior years of his life, there simmered a great need, not only to know his human fellows, but also to be known to them, to love them as he knew them, to be loved for who and what he was!

"Max Kintner!" he cried out at the top of his voice, ablaze with the conviction of this self-revelation. "Mrs. Max! Max Kintner and offspring, come out!" He screamed, "Sister Hanrahan, put your clothes back on and come out here! Drop that whip!" He yelled, "Megan! Come out! Bring your latest poem with you!" Bunce shouted at Professor Mayo's house, "Wendell Mayo, turn off the TV and come on out here! Bring your wife and daughters and beers for us all!"

"Come on out," Bunce called to his neighbors, "and talk to me!"

And Bunce waited, trembling, files in his shaking hands, for his neighbors to emerge, join him in the cul-de-sac street. Grubgeld and Paul Casey and Dan Baker would surely be there soon! He watched and waited, listened for approaching automobiles.

He thought it a shame he had not contacted his former wife and daughter, invited them, but he could do that later. They would all come together, Bunce was certain, and they would share—he would share with them all he had learned, and so give of himself to them all, was sure they would reciprocate, and in this sharing they would all come together in a new, profound humanity more wonderful, more mysterious than any had ever known before. They would all know the passion and peace they had sought, all unknowing, all the days of their lives!

"Oh," Bunce declaimed to the night's oncoming sky above Nottingham Estates, "Come out! Come out! Come out!"

ELEGY FOR ORRIN BODINE II

Old death is so beautiful—so very beautiful—
—Zelda Fitzgerald

Six weeks before his fiftieth birthday, Bodine's son, Orrin III, asked him, "So what's the birthday boy want for a present on the occasion of the big five-oh, Pops?" Bodine was so stricken with horror he had to close his eyes, breathe deeply, deliberately, before he could manage something that passed for a response. "Pops?" his son said when the silence expanded long enough to be remarkable.

"Whatever," Bodine said, opening his eyes but not looking at his son, not looking at anything. He did not see Orrin III, did not see Carla, his daughter-in-law, did not see his wife, Marylee, busy cutting coffee cake, setting out cups and saucers. "Anything," Bodine was able to say. "Nothing," and, "It's not like I'm a kid wants a new bike," and, "My age, it's another birthday, right?"

"Come off that," his son said, and laughed.

"At least give us a hint of an inkling, Dad," his daughter-in-law said.

"He's too shy," his wife said. "Or he's teasing. I go through this every year," she said.

Then his daughter-in-law, Carla, said something Bodine

didn't hear, and his wife said something about the coffee cake or the weather or Carla's earrings, and his son said something about money or the coffee cake or a birthday of his own he remembered. Bodine wasn't listening.

He thought to say what struck him when his son asked the question—Bodine thought to say: *This birthday I'll be the same age my father was when he died,* but said nothing, and shortly he felt able to eat coffee cake and drink coffee; he could nod and smile, muster all the expressions appropriate to a man fully engaged in conversation with his family. Eventually, by the time the dishes were cleared, his son and daughter-in-law on their way out, Bodine had begun to speak quite naturally and normally of what they had eaten, of weather and money and work and politics and what was on television yesterday, today, and tomorrow.

"So give us a ring if you get a flash about what you'd really like, Pops," Orrin III said as they left.

"He won't," Marylee said, "but I will sometime when he's not around to eavesdrop on me." Bodine found he could laugh with them as they all said goodbye.

The Big Five-Oh, Bodine thought as, locked in the bathroom, he scrutinized himself in the cabinet mirror. *Oh, Orry!* he thought. He thought: *Orry, didn't you see it coming? Did you think, Orry,* Bodine thought, *you'd live forever?* He examined himself in the mirror, noted the evidences.

He had his hair—oh, thank Whomever, he still had his hair! But it was shot with sickly grey, white swaths above each ear. And receded! Bodine tried to conjure the lush shocks that tumbled over his forehead, remembered the gunk he used as a boy and young man to slick it back out of his eyes, but he could not truly *see* that Orry-Who-Was-No-More. And thinned. There, in the unforgiving fluorescent light, he caught the gleam of his scalp revealed beneath the frail net of such hair as he had not lost, gradually, inexorably, to Time!

Oh, Orry!

My skin! Bodine thought. Wrinkled. *Wrinkled!* The receded expanse of his forehead slotted with permanent parallels, like a plowed field, indelible despite how tightly he stretched them with his fingers at his temples. Bodine leered defiantly at his image. At the corners of his muddy brown eyes—clouded with incipient cataracts?—twin fans cut deltas toward his ears, in each of which he saw, leaning close to the glass, sprouted clumps of stiff curled hairs—*white!* He admitted the reason he wore no moustache was because his beard had been white for years.

Bodine stepped back from the sink, assumed the most serious mien he could conceive, felt a tinge of nausea for the lines that ran like scars, one from each side of his thickening nose, unbroken, to frame his trembling chin.

Mercy! he thought, but steeled himself to record the disgusting roll of his dewlap, the textured crepe of his throat, the oversize pores pitting his face, the swollen pouch beneath each dull eye.

"Orry?" Marylee called from the other side of the locked door, "Are you taking up permanent residence?" Bodine flushed the commode, ran water in the sink, actually rinsed his hands for authenticity. Which was a mistake.

Drying them, he discovered the horny quality of his blunt nails, saw, as if for the first time, the revolting yellow-orange stain on the first and second fingers of his left hand that held the unfiltered cigarettes he'd smoked for thirty-three years— *why* had he ignored all the irrefutable discoveries of science!— discerned faint but tangible freckles dotting the backs of his hands—between the bluish bas-relief of veins—liver spots!

Bodine held out his hands, spread his fingers wide, formed

fists, cut figures of no symmetry in the air before him, remembered something he'd heard once, buried in his brain, erupting now to haunt him like the spectra of some evil done long ago he could now expiate only by sacrifice: *I looked down and saw my father's hand jutting out from my sleeve.*

Oh, Orry!

"Wasn't it nice Carla and Orry dropped over?" his wife said.

"It's funny, Marylee," Bodine said, "you'd think a man would feel different when he gets older, but I honestly don't feel the slightest bit different no matter what age I've been along the way."

"You're only as old as you feel, Orry," she said.

Bodine studied his wife when she wasn't looking; except for a little grey hair and some pounds around the middle, on her thighs, she didn't seem to have aged a day since he met her.

His wife said, "What ever are you doing with those old things? I thought you were going to take a nap," when she found Bodine in their bedroom, seated on the floor, surrounded by the photo albums and scrapbooks they kept on a high closet shelf, untouched for years.

He said, "I got a sudden hankering is all."

"Getting nostalgic in our dotage, are we?" Marylee said, smiled.

"No," Bodine said, and, "I said I just felt like looking through them, is that okay? And where's that box you toss pictures in?"

"What do you want with that mess, Orry?"

"I thought maybe I'd sort them out and stick them in if there's room in one of these," he said, and blew dust off the glossy green cover of a bulging album.

"You'll never make sense of that jumble," his wife said, went to the closet for the box in which they stored snapshots and clippings, personal letters, Christmas cards from old friends.

"I think I can if you'll give me a chance without interruption," Bodine said, regretting it because he could tell by the way she left the room after handing him the heavy box, his tone offended her.

Bodine began with the oldest of the photo albums, the ones his mother started and maintained, inherited when she died—a slow wasting death caused by a brain embolism, in an expensive nursing home—*I was forty-one when Mother left us,* Bodine thought. She was sixty-seven when she died; her death hurt, he remembered, but it had been expected, could be construed a merciful release, for her, for him.

Papa was just fifty, Bodine thought. It was not expected; Bodine was twenty-four, a newlywed—he rocked, seated Indian-style on his bedroom carpet, surrounded by scrapbooks and albums, with the revived shock of it, heard a distant keening sound, recognized the suffocated cry of his own renewed grief.

Papa! he thought, and, *Oh, Orry!*

Turning the stiff, dry pages, their original stark black gone dull, he saw his mother had done a marvelous job. She had sorted, mounted, captioned the pictures in the spider-web white ink of her graceful hand, imposed an order reflecting both genealogy and chronology. Bodine remembered her—his father away on business, selling—at work at their kitchen table, holding up each photograph for a last look before affixing the gummed corner tabs, licking them, pressing the picture to the page with a steady force—clucking her tongue now and again, whispering to herself, sighing occasionally—how, Bodine realized as he flipped and read, flipped, read, she must have grieved inwardly for her dead!

Here were Bodine's forebears, ancestors: maternal and paternal grandparents he'd never known—how like Bodine's father *his* father looked! *They look like me at my age!* Parents and grandparents, aunts and uncles and cousins, great-aunts and great-uncles, captured by cameras as infants, toddlers, boys and girls, youths, young-marrieds, parents, middle-aged, *old*! Caught, all of them, posed and candid, but nowhere in the family albums his mother compiled did Bodine find the slightest trace in any visage, smiling or solemn, of any awareness of their common mortality, no sign or signal that any, male or female, realized their impending necessary ends, that they should all come to people this encyclopedia of the deceased, anonymous save for his mother's ghostly white captions, laconic—insignificant.

Orrin's Aunt Amanda, Orrin Showing Off H.S. Graduation Suit, Orrin (Camp Grant? 1942?), Orrin With Baby.

And here was Bodine, curly headed, laughing, on Papa's lap! He turned the pages slowly, stared hard, torn between happy recognition of all the Orrin Bodine II selves and the conviction they were all utterly alien to the aging, doomed man—*Orry!*— who sat cross legged on a carpet with a volume, depicting dead people of no import, spread on his lap.

Orry Jr's First Pony Ride; Confirmation Day (Spoke His Piece Letter Perfect!); On My Honor—Bodine in his scout uniform, neckerchief, merit badges—*Out for A Spin!*—Bodine, greased pompadour, leaning, smirking out the driver's side window of his father's new company car—*Boot Camp*—Bodine, head shaved, looking like a child playing soldier in his OD uniform, Fort Leonard Wood—*Popular With All The Gals!*—Bodine between two girls he swore he'd never laid eyes on!—*Orry And M.L. (New Year's Eve)*—Bodine announced his engagement to his parents that night.

Bodine got as far as creating piles of snapshots and clippings from the large box Marylee found for him—a rough classification according to sequence, Orrin III's baby pictures, report cards, certificates; the family trio at the dinner table for Thanksgiving, beside Christmas trees; birthday parties—when he froze, slapped the albums shut, threw his stacks back in the box, crammed it all, in great haste, into the closet's deepest recess.

"All done down memory lane?" Marylee asked when he came to her in the laundry room, wash churning, dryer clicking.

"It'd take a genius to untangle that mare's nest," he lied.

What stopped him, made him gather and stash it all as if it were contaminated, contagious, was the sudden vision Bodine had: he saw someone—Marylee, his son, Carla, the possible grandchildren he'd not live to know, someone!—seated, on the floor, at a desk, leafing casually through the black pages, saying . . . saying, perhaps, *This is Orrin II. Do you remember him? You were too little when he died. Anyway, this is Orrin II, Orrin Jr., and back here, this is his father, the first Orrin, and this is his grandfather I think if I'm not mistaken. . . .*

Clobbered by this vision of himself, one more almost forgotten face in the chronicle of the departed, he was routed; he fled, but could not escape it.

"Marylee," he said, "when we have this birthday thing, Orry and Carla here and all, do me one favor and tell him ahead of time not to bring his camera, okay? I hate flashbulbs going off in my face, I always feel like an idiot getting my picture taken when I'm not looking for it. Okay?"

"What a thing to say, Orry!" his wife said.

The Tuesday night Orrin III called with the news, Bodine and his wife were in the den. Marylee was quilting, watching the late news. Bodine read the newspaper. When the phone rang, Marylee said, "Sit, I'll get it, you're reading and all the news is depressing anyhow." He waited until she was out of the den, talking on the hall extension—he could tell it was their son—before he turned quickly to the obituaries, let his wife's animated voice fade, scanned the day's local necrology.

There were so many! *I didn't know so many died on a weekday!* Bodine thought.

He skimmed the women, all but one of them in their seventies and eighties—*they live longer!*—the exception a wife and mother only thirty-six, the family requesting donations to a cancer fund in lieu of flowers. *Cancer,* he thought, vowed again to give up cigarettes. Save this one, the women all died in nursing homes and hospitals, the photographs of them long out of date, had survived their spouses, some of their children, by decades.

And there were men like this, one a veteran of World War I, one at age ninety-four, another, seventy, described as succumbing to a long illness, yet another, eighty-one, a former congressman, and a good dozen born within a few years either side of Bodine's father, his generation. *Papa!*

His wife's telephone voice, charged with excitement and laughter, was only a nagging echo in his ear as Bodine read slowly of the half-dozen peers who had, on this ordinary Tuesday of an ordinary week, suddenly exited this life.

David John Barczak, 48—died at his home, funeral arrangements pending . . . *Kevin Brendan Hawkins, 51*—of complications following routine surgery . . . *Robert Childers Parker, 49*—of injuries sustained while engaged in . . . *Grant Kent Williams, 50*—information received from authorities in the state of . . . *Charles James Revis, Jr., 53*—heart failure, stricken while. . . .

So many! Bodine thought, did not hear Marylee the first time she called him to the telephone, the newspaper trembling like an autumn leaf in his quivering, uncertain grasp. "Orry!" she said again. "Are you deaf suddenly? Come to the phone, your son has something to tell you!"

"Pops?" his son said to him, the receiver warm from his wife's ear against his; she beamed at him as he listened to his son. Orrin III's voice sounded metallic, very far away, as if it were a bad recording, a voice in a dream.

"I'm here. I was catching up on the paper," he said.

"Pops, I'm sorry to call so late, but I've got some news. I told Mother the details, so she can tell you more, but I just wanted to tell you myself. I'm going to be a daddy, Pops. You're going to be a grampa before you see another birthday after this next one. Pops?" his son said when Bodine said nothing.

"That's some news," he said, then had to smile at his wife when she reached out and put a hand on his arm. "That's swell," Bodine said, and made himself put his free arm around his wife's shoulder. "Really terrif," he said.

"I thought you'd be tickled," Orrin III said, and, "We're both sky high. I don't know if you know how hard we've been trying. We could have waited to tell you, make it a sort of extra birthday present for you, but I wanted to now. Hey, Pops, Carla says love, we're calling her folks now. Tell Mother love for me, huh?"

"Bye, bye," Bodine said, "I'm thrilled," he said, then hung up the receiver, and then he returned Marylee's embrace while he searched for the right things to say, questions to ask, rehearsed the smile he'd need to show her.

"If it's a boy," Marylee said, "I'll wager dollars to donuts we have a little Orrin the Fourth to love!"

"I'll pass on that bet," Bodine said, cold with the vision of his son pointing out names and faces to his grandson as they sat, somewhere, with a family photo album between them.

They kept dying. Bodine turned first to the obits, taking the daily paper the moment he returned from work, sneaking off to the den to tally the count of his peers who had shuffled—or jumped or been yanked or thrown!—off this mortal coil, while Marylee cooked his supper. He watched the late television news with her each night, steeled himself to avoid flinching when, almost every time, there was a segment, complete with capsule biography, of some celebrity's demise: a Hollywood leading man felled by AIDS, a Middle East spiritual leader slain by a crazed gunman, a tycoon incinerated in the collision of two airplanes, an All-American athlete overdosed on drugs, a regional politician with tangible national prospects gone only weeks after an operation to excise a tumor, the ubiquitous coronaries. . . .

So many! Bodine thought.

"You're very subdued," his wife said.

"I can't hardly scintillate all the time, Marylee," he told her, and, "Once in a blue moon a person has to charge his batteries if he wants to last, don't you think?"

Their family physician said, "Long time no see you, Orrin. I always ask your good wife after you when she comes in, but I figure if I don't hear from you, nothing's hurting."

Bodine said, "I just thought it'd be a good time to get a good going over."

"Ounce of prevention," his doctor said, and, "Anything in specific causing concern?"

"No. I'm turning fifty here soon, so get the plumbing checked out is all."

"Better safe than," the doctor said, and, "Are you that old, Orrin?" and looked at Bodine's file, grinned, said, "So you are! Tempis fugit. Any complaints, Orrin?" he said. "I wish more men took the trouble. Well," he said, took his pen from his smock's pocket, uncapped it, "let's us get you the whole lox while we're at it, seeing as we see you so seldom. Knock wood," he said, rapped the wall of the examination cubicle with his knuckles.

"I actually feel fine," Bodine said.

And he was. Bodine's blood and urine specimens proved untainted, their components within the parameters of normal proportion, their respective flows unclogged, well regulated by heart and kidneys, and his heart's graphed trail was steady, even. His lungs cast no ominous shadows, all vital organs duly certified operative.

"So I'm fine?" Bodine asked.

"As good as you could hope, Orrin," his doctor said. "Your prostate's a little firm to the touch, but that's to be expected. That smoker's cough won't get better unless you knock it off, but I don't have to repeat what you know better. All in all, you could watch your diet, and your muscle tone's nothing to shout about, you could do with exercise—try walking if you don't like to perspire—I feel good about it," he said, closing Bodine's file.

"So I'm fine."

"For a man your vintage, Orrin, yes," his doctor said.

"So do I get a report or is it a state secret?" Marylee said.

"I'm fine," Bodine told her. "Normal. Clean bill. I should get more exercise and quit smoking, and it's okay to have a martini when I feel like it, oh yes, and avoid fatty foods for cholesterol, which I already knew."

"That's wonderful," she said. "I'm glad you finally got it in your noggin to go see him, I used to think you were frightened of doctors and medicine."

"I knew I was fine before I went," Bodine said, "and I am, so that's that."

It wasn't. Bodine knew better. He wasn't *fine* at all!

When he woke each morning, Marylee already up and dressing, his brain was fogged with more than sleep; Bodine had to grope his way through a miasma's residue, the backwash of unrecollected nightmares, to clutch the words she spoke to him, his vision blurred, as if the motor of his senses balked at running after the long, deep dormancy of slumber. His body, as he sat up in bed, swung his leaden legs onto the floor, was stiff with aches, tweaked with shooting pains lasting only milliseconds. When he stood, he swayed, giddy. When he spoke, his voice was alien, clotted with smoker's rheum. In response to Marylee's "Good morning, Merry Sunshine!" he barely croaked. Bodine dared not face his day's first face in the mirror, shaved like a blind man, eyes closed.

I'm not fine! he thought.

He heard whistles and wheezes in his breathing, suffered sideaches when he sat too long, experienced inexplicable tingling sensations in his forearms and spasms of numbness in his fingers and toes, episodes of soft roaring in his ears, dull headaches between his eyes, sore joints, fits of itching, sudden sweats, the feeling his blood raced, heart thumped, acid stomach and explosive belching and farting after eating even bland foods.

Hell of a lot doctors know! Bodine thought.

Not without a fight! Bodine vowed.

"Orry," his wife said, "this sort of comes at me out of the blue."

"The doctor," he told her, "told me to watch my diet. I told you that, right? Is it too much to ask?" So Marylee eliminated meat from his meals, did not complain—though she muttered to herself it was silly as she stood over the stove—when he brought her health foods to prepare: brown rice, dried kelp, organically grown fruit and vegetables, stone-ground flour, unadulterated peanut butter. She said nothing when he came home from a shopping trip with vitamin supplements and protein wafers. But he caught her staring when he combined blackstrap molasses, wheat germ, and brewer's yeast in their blender with coconut and papaya juice.

"I wouldn't stand close enough to smell that goop much less drink it," Marylee said.

"If all of us," Bodine said, "maintained our bodies like we do a new car we buy, we'd be the better off for it," and swallowed, pinching his eyes shut at the taste.

"Can you give me at least a clue of what you're up to, Orrin?" Marylee said when she came on him in their bedroom, straining midway through a pushup, face red and contorted, arms trembling, sweat dripping off the end of his nose. Bodine had to catch his breath after collapsing on his stomach, spoke, muffled, into the carpet's nap.

"Trying," he said, "to increase my cardiovascular efficiency," and listened, long after she left the bedroom, to the whirring of his heart he felt vibrate all the way down to the tips of his toes.

"May I be so bold as to inquire as to what this purchase entailed?" Marylee asked, held up the charge receipt from the sporting goods store; Bodine had forgotten she kept the checkbook, paid the monthly bills.

"Shoes."

"Shoes?"

"Running shoes."

"*Running* shoes?"

"And sweats and a headband and a supporter and cushion-sole socks and a velcro thing you wear on your wrist to hold your house key and money and whatever."

"I give up!" Marylee said.

"I haven't," Bodine told her, disarmed when she did not continue the conversation.

I can do this! he thought as he jogged through his neighborhood. The early morning air flavored with a thick mist, the day's first light suffused with promise, the empty streets—he felt strong and aggressive, as if he were the first man in the world, had been here since Creation, destined to know and command it into eternity. *I can hack it!* Bodine thought, and welcomed the sweat that popped out on his skin, the first pangs of fatigue climbing his legs, the huff of his breathing as he started up a long incline. Bodine waved at a fellow jogger who sprinted past him, a young woman running like a precision machine.

"The secret's starting slow and working your way up to some distance, Uncle!" she called over her shoulder, disappeared over the crest of the hill, her slapping feet an echo.

"I'll make it!" he cried into the fog that closed behind her, surprised at the whine of uncertainty in his voice, a wailing. But he did not.

"How far'd you go?" his wife asked as she unlaced his shoes for him.

"Mile," Bodine groaned. "Half a mile. I lost track," he said, sprawled on their bed, feet dangling.

"You look like the last dog hung, Orry," she said. "Get in the shower; it'll revive you."

"It's not fair, Marylee," he said, "when I was in shape for this stuff I didn't need it."

"Is this your version of mid-life crisis, Orry?" she asked. Bodine forgave her, knew she was trying to joke it away for his sake. All that day on the job, he felt drained of energy, astounded he did not simply collapse in place.

Too late, Orry! Bodine thought. His health diet upset his digestion, deranged his bowels, left him weak and ravenous; he dreamed of junk food. Pushups and situps made his muscles scream, and jogging appeared to have permanently damaged his spine and ankles. He lost some weight, but this made his face sallow and drawn in the bathroom mirror, skin blanched. He forced himself to look at himself. *Too late!* Bodine thought, and flushed the commode, ran the sink taps to conceal the sound of his weeping.

Bodine had no idea his son was coming, learned only from him that Marylee invited Orry III to please stop by and talk with his father. Bodine was alone in the den, monitoring the late news for word of who'd gone that day, absorbed, unaware his wife had gone to answer the doorbell. He heard their voices, whispering just out in the hall, but blocked them out—there was a famous entertainer, rushed to a hospital earlier in the week, Bodine had a hunch wouldn't make it.

"Orrin," his wife said from the doorway, "your son's here."

"Great," and, "Hi, Orry," he said without looking away from the television.

"How you doing, Pops?" his son said.

"He wants to talk to you, Orrin," Marylee said.

"Sure thing. Come on in and sit down, kid," he said, then looked up at his wife and son when the news cut to a commercial; surprised by their solemn expressions, he made himself smile, held it on his face even when his wife scooted off down the hall, his son entered the den, sat on the ottoman in front of Bodine's recliner. "Slide over just a hair, Orry," Bodine said, "you're blocking the screen. I want to catch something, it'll be over in a second, we'll gab."

"Pops," Orry III said, and, "Dad, Mother's telling me some things I—" but the news cut back in, a curt spot following up on the seriously ill entertainer, reported now in critical condition, intensive care, an on-scene statement from the celebrity's agent thanking everyone for all the messages of sympathy and good wishes.

"Did you hear what I said, Pops?" his son said, but Bodine didn't speak until the spot ended, the news cut to the national weather map.

"I went to see him in movies when I was your age, Orry," Bodine said. "He was one of my father's all-time favorite singers, I probably never told you that. You never knew my father," he said to his son.

"Pops," Orry III said, leaned forward on the ottoman, put his hands on Bodine's shoulders, forced him to make eye-contact. "I said Mother's telling me you're acting . . . *strange*."

"How *strange*?"

"Like now," his son said, "not hearing when she talks to you, just sort of odd generally, I guess, besides this business of buying jogging gear all of a sudden, refusing to eat what she makes for supper, withdrawing sort of. Pops?"

Bodine looked at his son. He ran over the things he could say to explain it all away, how it was Marylee's imagination, or a lie he could spin about money worries, problems at the office, but he thought: *Tell somebody.* "Pops?" his son said again.

Bodine said, "Do you know how my father, your grandfather, died, Orry?"

"What?"

"I know I never told you. Why would I? Your mother knows, but I bet we never talked about it, why would we?"

"I'm not following, Pops."

"My father, I called him Papa from the time I was a child, was this perfectly healthy, happy, successful man. All his life. My memories of him are him smiling and laughing a lot, he seemed like such a big, large man to me, I suppose it seemed that way from when I was a small boy looking up to him, huh? He was actually only average, my size. Anyway," he said when his son said nothing, "you have to grasp the idea he was this *permanent* person in my life, who I was, there from the start, and it felt to me he'd always be there—"

"Hey, Pops," Orry III said, but Bodine continued.

"Then one day, he was just fifty, he was out on some errand,

and he stopped for gas and went to the restroom while the guy fills his tank and what-all, we got all this from the guy himself. My papa didn't come out of the john, the gas station guy finally went and knocked, they had to call a locksmith to open the door—"

"Pops—"

"—my papa died in there, Orry. Perfectly happy and strong, he goes in the bathroom to use the john, he drops on the floor, dead like he'd been shot, hit by a lightning bolt. Aneurism. In the toilet of a damn gas station, just fifty, no warnings, not the slightest—"

"Dad," his son said, "why are you crying?" Bodine put his hand to his face, felt his tears on his cheek, pulled out his handkerchief, wiped his eyes, blew his nose, cleared his throat, coughed. "I'm sorry about your father, but I don't get what's bothering you," his son was saying. "I'm sorry if I don't get the point. Do you think it'd be a good idea to maybe get some professional counseling help?" he said.

Bodine let him talk, got hold of himself, and when his son was talked out, said he was sorry, said people got depressed for no reason sometimes, said Marylee made too much of things, said he'd be fine, and eventually Bodine and his son stood up, hugged each other, and Bodine asked how Carla was handling pregnancy, was she ill mornings or getting crazy craves yet?

"I guess I'm glad Mother asked us to talk," Orrin III said.

Too late, Bodine thought, *too late even to tell someone!*

"Mirror, mirror on the wall," Marylee said when she walked past the bathroom door, glimpsed Bodine, hands braced on the sink, his face only inches from the glass.

He jumped back, said, "I had a blackhead."

"Vanity, vanity," his wife said in a sing-song, her voice fading as she went on into their bedroom. Bodine closed the bathroom door, locked it, went back to the mirror. *Cosmetics,* he thought.

They could do wonders! Hair implants, take plugs from the back of his neck, set them like budding shoots in his scalp, give him a thatch thick as a lion's mane! Dye. They had formulas that worked gradually, nobody noticed the tell-tale grey vanishing. Skin tucks, face lifts! Cut and draw his hide back and up, no scars, erase the troughs in his forehead, deflate the bags under his eyes, sculpt a sharp, confident chin! And the miracle oils women used to restore their glow, applications that bestowed a vacationer's tan—Bodine could remake himself as he had once been, create a visage he'd exult to confront each morning!

"Are we still the fairest in the land?" Marylee asked him with a sweet smile when they met in the breakfast nook. She stopped smiling when he told her, roughly, he didn't know what she was talking about.

Who would I be fooling? Bodine thought over his bacon and eggs.

Seventeen days before Bodine's fiftieth birthday, his neighbor died suddenly. When he drove up to his house from the office, he saw the ambulance in the driveway next door, paramedics wheeling out the stretcher, sheet strapped down over the corpse. Marylee was weeping. "What?" Bodine said.

"Orry," she sniffled, "he just went. I've been over there until just now, her daughter came, she's a wreck!"

"What?" Bodine said, and, "What killed him? Stop crying and tell me, Marylee."

"God knows," his wife said. "Stroke possibly. She's so hysterical, her daughter got their doctor to prescribe something. He just fell over and laid there twitching, he couldn't speak, she's not strong enough to lift him, his eyes rolled up and he tried to talk but it was like he was swallowing his tongue, then he was just gone! Oh, Orry!" Marylee said, and began to cry harder, and Bodine had to hold her, comfort her before she could answer him.

"How old was he, Marylee?"

"I don't know," she said, and then she said, "his early sixties at most. But he was such a vigorous man! I don't know why I can't get a grip on myself," his wife said, "we weren't all that close. Oh, Orry!"

Orry! Bodine thought.

He considered more profound measures. Surgery! They could go inside your body, Bodine thought, perform marvels! The glands of young adult primates to replace the ones wearing out, inject hormones, cells scraped from unborn sheep fetuses! And medical engineering, artificial kidneys and hearts, microscopic computer gizmos that saw like eyes, heard like ears, caps that made your teeth look like polished ivory! Arms and legs operated by cables attached to muscles, indistinguishable from the real thing! Human organ transplants! Rejuvenation clinics in Switzerland, Mexico, southern California!

Impossible, Bodine thought, *the cost*!

The anniversary of his birth a week and a half away, Bodine came to work, noticed immediately something was wrong. No typewriters clacked, no phones were in use, salesman and secretaries and file clerks huddled in knots of three and four, talking softly, expressionless. "What gives?" he asked his secretary.

"Oh, Mr. Bodine," she said, looked away, found her purse, took out a hankie, dabbed at her eyes. "It's Mr. Kaminsky!" and then she truly had to dry her teary eyes.

"How? When?" he said.

"Did you already know?" she asked. "I just now heard when I came in this morning. It was just last night."

"I assumed," Bodine said. "How, exactly?" he said.

"It's terrible," she said, "he stopped out on the freeway to help somebody's car broke down, a drunk sideswiped them both, they never knew what hit them. Oh, nobody feels like working today, Mr. Bodine! He's got three kids I think, I met his wife's so sweet the one time at the party, he was only forty years old, somebody said, I didn't even think he was that old!"

"I can understand that," Bodine said. "Listen," he told her, "go home if there's nothing pressing right now, okay? I'm going home myself, I don't feel all that hot myself. Okay?"

Cryogenics, he thought. Get yourself in deep freeze, suspended animation, like a long sleep minus the bad dreams! Hole up and wait until technology cured everything. Who knew the possibilities? Get frozen, a contract to be thawed out in, say, ten years, wake up and check things out—if it wasn't safe yet, go back into hibernation another decade! You could wait it out forever!

Bodine imagined himself frozen, a vault inside a huge building, maybe underground to guard against disasters, a generator humming, sub-zero gasses swirling in tubes . . . then he saw it like a coffin, buried, a mausoleum, and thought: what if the generator failed? What if there was an earthquake? What if the contract was broken on a technicality? Nuclear war! Then he imagined himself, buried in his coffin under tons of radioactive rubble, thawing, rotting—*No!*

"Pops?" his son's voice said in the receiver.

"Hi. I thought I wouldn't hear from you until you and Carla come over for the big doings. Sunday?"

"Of course it's Sunday, Pops. No, hey, I just called about what we talked about? You know. Did you by any chance go see anybody like we mentioned?"

"No," Bodine said. "Your mother putting a bee in your bonnet again, is she?"

"Don't put me on the spot that way, Pops. Pops? I hear you stopped going to work?"

"I've got the time coming to me," Bodine said.

His son exhaled loudly. "Can't you tell me anything, Pops? I'm your son," he said.

"No," Bodine said, and, "See you and Carla Sunday."

"Right, Sunday," Orrin III said.

"Lord willing, etcetera," Bodine said.

Sunday morning, having lived half a century, Bodine didn't get up when Marylee called him. When she asked him if he meant to sleep half the day away, he said, "I just feel like a little extra snoozing."

"No wonder," she said, "I felt you tossing half the night."

"I won't be long," he said, turned toward the wall, pulled the covers over his head. He had not slept, but he was not tired. He had been afraid to fall asleep, feared the dreams he might have, that he might die in his sleep. Through the long night, Bodine's imagination ran like filmstrip, visions of his possible deaths.

If he got up to go for a drink of water, he might stumble in the dark, fall, break his neck; if he lay too long in one position, rigid, his circulation might slow, fail to sufficiently nourish his brain and lungs; if he thrashed, he might wake Marylee, strangle on whatever words came to his throat to lie to her.

It was mid-morning when Bodine sensed his wife in their bedroom again; he played possum, held his breath while she stood watching him, grateful he didn't have to cough until after she quietly left. He thought he heard her on the telephone a little later.

He tried, a last time, to resolve to get up, go as far into this day as he was allowed, but dared not. Bodine imagined dying in the midst of sitting up, throwing back the covers, Marylee finding him sprawled half-off their bed; he imagined dying in the bathroom, naked in the shower, bleeding from a gash where his head struck the edge of the tub; he saw himself die while dressing, ridiculous with his trousers halfway up his legs, shirt unbuttoned; he saw himself as far as the kitchen, the breakfast nook, electrocuted by a freak short circuit in the coffee percolator, asphyxiated by a crumb of toast lodged in his windpipe, his head dropping into his eggs—*No!* Bodine thought.

Then he heard the doorbell, voices, Orrin III and Carla, Marylee, his wife telling them something was wrong. They approached the bedroom, then retreated, voices rising, argument, debating what to do. Bodine wrapped the covers close all around himself, shut his eyes, strove to turn off his hearing. Bodine wasn't moving. Nobody, nothing, would budge him!

In the unbroken darkness behind his sealed eyes, Orrin Bodine II held his breath, limbs stiffened, went deaf to the world's ephemeral sounds, focused the concentrated whole of his sentience and sensibilities on the phenomenon of his mortal flesh. Bodine poised, waited on whatever form and substance his imminent termination might assume.

THE APOTHEOSIS OF NEDDIE HACKE

ℰℛ

> *My father made your yoke heavy,*
> *and I will add to your yoke. . . .*
>
> I Kings 12.14

Hacke wasn't sure he actually *wanted* to be the new Dean of Arts & Science; Jake Gibbs, Vice-President for Academic Affairs—number two man in the university, right under and directly responsible only to The Prez himself—decided him. "I think," Gibbs said when the subject came up innocently enough during a routine budget conference in the V.P.'s office, "it's traditionally pro forma for an acting or interim incumbent to stand for the job, Ned."

Hacke said, "I wouldn't want to look like I'm trying to slip in the chair sideways." Vice-President Gibbs only smiled, then turned back to the budget. It was enough; Hacke had his cue.

Dr. Ned Hacke, Associate Professor of History, Acting Interim Dean of Arts & Science—warming the chair for the past month, since Dean Sammy Holly took indefinite leave without pay to head up state education for the new governor—listened, responded appropriately when it was appropriate, but his real attention focused on trying to read Jake Gibbs's message.

Was Hacke being set up, recruited to swell the ranks, the list of interviewed candidates the administration had to file with

Affirmative Action? Was he being told to trot through the motions, a stalking horse for some predetermined crony of Gibbs's or The Prez's, a sacrificial decoy to make some token female or black look good?

Or was the Vice-President's casual remark a coded signal the position was Hacke's for the asking, a reward richly deserved for long and faithful services rendered, Gibbs's version of a wink to tell him the fix was in, all he had to do was put in a perfunctory bid?

Hacke couldn't figure it; nobody figured Jake Gibbs, which was why he was the university's number two, had been for over twenty years—nobody could read the Vice-President for Academic Affairs.

On one hand, Gibbs *looked* authoritative. He was regally tall, wore the right clothes, even effected a sporty touch younger than his years, mouthed the abstractions of Academese fluently, showed his teeth a lot in what passed for a cheerful mien, wore glasses thick enough it was impossible to tell if his eyes twinkled merrily or sparked with malevolence. And he was *slick!* Hacke had never known him to answer a query candidly or directly, never seen him telegraph a punch; Jake Gibbs kept the axe he wielded at The Prez's pleasure behind his back, up his sleeve, under his coat.

Vice-President for Academic Affairs Jake Gibbs even practiced the knee-jerk common touches: he first-named everyone except The Prez, came out from behind his massive desk to sit on the sofa with whoever visited his office, unobtrusively picked up the tabs for the lunches he shared with his deans, glad-handed candidates touring campus to interview for faculty positions, never declined invitations to present awards or just grace a dais, to deliver a canned keynote address to a student organization.

On the other hand, Gibbs would, Hacke thought, have been a

university president himself, were it not for a few tragic flaws, cracks in the edifice: he wore a hearing aid, a thick plastic plug jammed in his ear, and when he stood, his height was undercut by an unusually protruding belly, goiterlike, that rendered him a little silly, and, of course, if anyone actually tried to listen to his pronouncements on higher education, he revealed only platitudes at best, at worst, abysmal ignorance.

When the Vice-President sighed, glanced at his wristwatch, raised his bushy brows, telling Hacke the discussion was over, they shook hands—Gibbs had an administrator's handclasp down pat: firm, short, dry, sincerely formal—Hacke tried to look through the man's distorting spectacles for a clue in the obscured eyes, found nothing.

Dr. Ned Hacke left Central Administration, crossed campus to Arts & Science, still wondering if he had been tapped for the deanship, or was he but designated the pawn of a cynical, manipulative bureaucracy? Would he, in a few weeks, be the new Dean of Arts & Science, or just another sucker, used, humiliated, doubly a fool for volunteering his neck on the block of expediency that was the university's animating principle?

Whatever, when Hacke reached his office complex, he told his secretary no calls, no appointments, closed his door, and spent the rest of the day at labor, drafting his letter presenting himself as a candidate for the vacant position.

In his fortieth year, Hacke's appearance and demeanor revealed the sort of child, boy, and young man he'd been.

Neddie Hacke had to have been small, undersize from birth, shorter and lighter, more frail than any of his peers, and so, naturally, always on the periphery of games and friendship. Given no less than average intelligence and the self-conscious-ness an only child inherits from his parents' undiluted atten-tion, Neddie made as much strength as possible from the vulnerability dealt him, arbitrarily, by Nature. Earlier than most boys unable to compete for dominance and leadership roles, he resorted to conflict avoidance and taciturnity as tactics, took anonymity for his prevailing strategy.

Neddie Hacke was the sort of kid his classmates never, years later, remembered. He'd be hard to locate in one of those grade school group pictures: stuck out on the end of the middle row, where his pale face, mousy hair, and nondescript clothes tended to blend him with the dull buff gym wall behind the bleachers on which the photographer posed them, or tucked between two grinning or glowering thugs twice his size, eclipsed by their broad shoulders and already distended bellies, or placed in a rank of girls about the same height, where his even, expression-less features assumed an androgynous cast.

If a classmate, years later, were to examine the picture, show-ing his children what their daddy looked like in the fourth or fifth grade, he'd be bound to say of Neddie Hacke, *Now him, that little twerp, I'm damned if I can think of his name!*

By the time he reached high school, Neddie would have his mode of confronting existence down cold: silence, distance, and the transformation of his spontaneous feelings to an inward, objectified puzzle, a narcissistic core of the self he isolated, de-fined, and then stifled in the interest of survival. Since he posed no masculine threat to the boys, they had no need to torment him, which amounted to a kind of bland popularity, even as it precluded the intensity of close comradeship. Since Neddie was barred from conventional avenues of sexual expression, the girls accepted him, even rather liked him, platonically. And since he had to find some means of establishing a sense of self-worth—and had to justify his parents' unthinking approval—he was alertly attentive in classes, did all his homework on time, and earned the superior grades given enthusiastically by his grateful teachers. Unable to wholly deny his basic need for some sort of human interaction, however superficial, he was active in debate, student government, and History Club.

Neddie Hacke's high school graduation portrait showed a nice-looking boy, not a hair out of place, his expression so solemn as to resemble the visages of department store dummies, eyes as deliberately vacant as a taxidermist's marbles, thin lips locked, chin raised just a tad—the only evidence that this pasty pudding of a youth harbored a chilled determination nobody was ever going to see him inadvertently reveal. Graduated, with a few other misfits and the handful of truly gifted in his school's scholastic top 5 percent, he was as surely college bound as if God called him personally to higher learning.

Neither ambitious nor accomplished enough to enter a first-rate university, Ned—he could no longer bear to think of himself as *Neddie,* winced even when his mother persisted in so addressing him—elected a large public institution; anyone could fit in, disappear there. Ignorant of and uninterested in science, confused and embarrassed by art and literature, he vacillated among the cafeteria offerings in the social sciences, chose history as his major because, at least with respect to ancient and classical times, it seemed permanently fixed, exhibited none of the disturbing, trendy flux of sociology, none of the fuzzy mythology with which anthropology was permeated, less quirky precision than the study of language. Thus it was, among the Greek and Roman ruins, in the tedious and yet esoteric scholarship attendant, Ned Hacke found his professional vocation.

His pattern and personality now jelled for life. Solitary, unresponsive, diligent, competent to the degree required, he walked the sure and certain channels of graduate study, emerged with a doctorate at a time when there were still jobs in his discipline, was hired by a land grant school only a shade less distinguished than his mediocre alma mater, was promoted, then tenured.

Gordon Weaver

Ned's hair greyed prematurely, which gave him a patina of dignity, and the inexorable accumulation of twenty-five extra pounds bestowed an aura of substance on him that almost compensated for his diminutive stature. His bachelorhood stimulated a brief rash of gossip that he was a fag, but his evident celibacy squelched this in time; he was accepted, correctly, as asexual.

Dr. Ned Hacke might have served all his days in the obscurity of his lackluster department, almost content at having managed so well against the odds of the endowment Fate handed him, had it not been for a chain of events so coincidental, so unpredictable, their meaning emerged for him only after their effects were manifest. And these events might have had no telling effect for Ned Hacke, Ph.D., save for the secret resolve, not just to endure, but to prevail, he nurtured from well before the hint of it surfaced in that set of his jaw discernible in his high school graduation portrait.

"The word on campus," Weber told him, "is you're just pro forma."

"That's about the size of it," Hacke said.

"You telling me you don't really want it?" Weber said, and, "Come off it, Neddie! I can see you salivating."

"I'd hardly put it that way," Hacke said.

"*You* wouldn't," Weber said, "which is why you're a candidate. I *would*," he said, "because I know you too well, besides which I don't have administrative ambitions, which means I'm free to say what I think." Weber leered at him, and Hacke let himself smirk, just a little.

Weber, a tenured full professor of English, was the closest thing to a friend Ned Hacke had in his life. They'd met when both were new on the faculty, assistant professors fresh out of grad school, members of a bunch that gathered on the campus greensward on Sunday mornings to play touch football with the graduate students. It took Hacke a while to figure out why he liked this man.

"So you're saying I haven't got a Chinaman's chance?"

"*I'm* not saying that, your competition is, Neddie."

From the first day, Weber put the needle on him. When he called elaborate play patterns in the huddle, he said, *Hacke— Ned is it? Okay, Neddie-boo, you go out short. Also, don't go more then ten yards over scrimmage, then curl back, I'll hit you if I can't find a tall receiver.* It became a standing joke—*Hacke, go out short!*—Hacke had to laugh along until he could gracefully stop coming out on Sundays to play.

When Weber was tenured and promoted early—his scholarship had a national reputation, and his teaching evaluations blew out the top of the scale—he called Hacke to crow, said, *See what happens sometimes when you work hard, Neddie? Not to worry, you'll get yours when the time comes, sycophancy always pays out in the end, keep the faith, Neddie!* When Hacke got the chair in History, in the midst of the chaos of the Orry Frank scandal, Weber said, *Way to go, Neddie! I was beginning to worry you wouldn't get tenure, but this cinches it, they can't can two department heads in a row, even in your fifth-rate shop, huh?*

"So what are you saying, Weber?"

"I'm saying you're the dark horse. I'm saying Jakie Gibbs touted it to you just in case the declared candidates all prove unacceptable."

Why he liked Weber, Hacke was sometimes able to admit to himself, was because he was everything Hacke wasn't. Weber was tall, lean, handsome, masculine. Weber was a proven scholar; his articles appeared only in peer-reviewed journals, his book-length study of Joyce stirred controversy, won an award. He was a dynamic classroom teacher who seemed to actually *like* students, had a large following among them. Weber was married, had children. Weber said whatever came to his mind, spared nobody, observed none of the conventional academic pieties and hypocrisies. Weber was, Hacke more than once confessed to himself, just the sort of man he, Ned Hacke, would like to have been had he not been forced to be who and what he was.

Hacke found himself, sitting in the student union cafeteria over coffee with him, feeling equally fond and afraid of the English professor.

"You have any idea how many outside applicants they must have by now?" Hacke said. "It's a national search, they're bound to get some hotshots in the pile."

"Oh, Neddie!" Weber said. "Oh, Neddie-boo! Are you that naive, or are you just pulling my chain? You of all people should know it's got to be an in-house choice, right?"

"I don't follow that logic."

"So you say. Look around you. Check out the gang of dorks we refer to euphemistically as our beloved administration."

"So?"

"So, dorks, nerds, semicompetents, time-servers, trimmers, orifice osculators, all *home grown,* Neddie!"

"The Prez wasn't."

"That's *state* politics, Board of Regents scams. Besides The Prez. Gibbs on down, all selected from within, the reason for which is or ought to be obvious to even you, Neddie."

"Indulge me," Hacke said.

Weber said, "Neddie, do I have to draw you pictures? Man, they start bringing in outsiders, they might goof, get some now and then with actual *ability,* actual records of *achievement*! No, Neddie, it's the incest ethos, right? Elevate from within the fold, you *know* you can count on their total unsuitability for the work, right?" Hacke made himself laugh to divert Weber's intensity.

"So how'd you rate my chances?" he asked.

Weber said, "You're my personal odds-on fave rave, Neddie. If there was a pool I'd lay my cash on you!"

"Why's that?"

"Neddie," Weber said, "are you fishing for an insult?"

"I can always count on you," Hacke said.

"I hope so," Weber said, and, "Neddie, even with the formidable competition of dufus misfits you face, you're *clearly* the least qualified! Neddie," he said, "unless you screw up and do something stupid like teach well or publish or come out with an idea that really addresses a problem, son, you're a shoe-in!"

Weber laughed, and Hacke laughed with him. "I mean," Weber said, "history's on your side, right, Neddie?" Hacke liked the English professor so well at the moment he didn't even cringe when he called him Neddie, the way he did when even his mother said it.

When the Orry Frank scandal hit the fan, Ned Hacke was more surprised than his History Department colleagues, who all seemed to know something was simmering. Hacke was preoccupied with his upcoming tenure review, depressed at the all-but-certain prospect he'd be cut loose, shoved out the door, thrown on the job market where, in the five years since he received his doctorate, positions in the humanities and social sciences had evaporated, the nation suffering a glut of Ph.D.'s scrambling for the rare openings. Dr. Orry Frank, his department head, was at the heart of the problem.

In five years, Hacke managed to publish only two short book reviews, neither of them peer-juried, his teaching evaluations were only satisfactory—students wrote things like: *Dr. Hacke is a nice man, but his lectures put me to sleep; this course could be interesting if the instructor could relate the material to real life; who cares about the dumb greeks and Rome and all!*—and failed election to any standing departmental committees. Orry Frank scorned ancient and classical history, defined his department's focus as recent and contemporary regionalism, and believed voluminous publication, no matter how trivial the subjects, was the only way to earn the higher administration's favorable regard.

Hacke felt doomed. Weber asked him, "Have you sat down with old Orry and talked about it? Tell him you can't have a History Department without at least one ancient-classical man, hell, lie to him, tell him you're at work on a definitive revisionary interpretation of traditional scholarship!"

"I haven't got a prayer, Weber," Hacke said. "You know Frank, he cranks out those biographies of guys who founded chain stores and junk annotated editions of pioneers' personal letters. Christ, Orry goes around referring to tenure review as nut-cutting time! I'm finished," he said, "I'll have to try to get on as a textbook salesman or apply for the federal civil service!"

"Hope for a miracle," Weber said, but Hacke couldn't.

Then he got one.

Orry Frank and one of his cronies, another regional historian, got caught with their fingers in the till, juggling Development Foundation funds earmarked to support research efforts; they siphoned off only a few thousand dollars, but it was too blatant to let pass by calling it an administrative mistake, the way they did when one of the Foundation trustees paid his babysitter from travel monies. It broke the night before Halloween. Hacke answered his doorbell, a bag of candy in his hand, ready to dole out to the trick-or-treaters, but it wasn't a gang of costumed kids—it was Weber, made up like a zombie; he said he was supposed to be one of the tenured dead. He said, "I am the good angel of unexpected mercies come to save Neddie Hacke from a confrontation with real life!"

"Are you drunk?" Hacke asked.

The Apotheosis of Neddie Hacke

When he could stop laughing, Weber told him, "Even as I speak to you, your beloved Orry Frank and his buddy boy are, upon orders direct from The Prez himself, cleaning out their desks. I hear they've already lined up jobs with a textbook publisher, but that's probably a nasty rumor."

"You're smashed, Weber!"

"I will be if you'll invite me in and offer me libations," he said, and, "Far from it. Worse, I'm amazed! Astounded! Can you believe it, Neddie, they actually *fired* somebody, two of them, and all they did was steal money from the university? Hey, there's hope for this profession yet, Neddie me boy!"

It was Hacke's miracle. When the History faculty couldn't get past the in-fighting of competing factions, Dean Sammy Holly called him in. Dean Holly said, "I want you to head up History's shop for me, Ned. I want you to get in that chair and sit on it, and I want you to make peace and quiet for me, understand? I want Jake Gibbs and The Prez off my neck, and I want an end to articles in the papers and on TV about professors in my college embezzling. I want History to *teach history* to students and stop squabbling, and that's all I want! Can you do that for me, Ned?"

"I'm an untenured assistant professor, Dean," Hacke said. Dean Sammy Holly waved his hand in the air, as if shooing a pesky gnat.

"That's the least of your worries," he said. "I'll take care of that instanter," the Dean said. "I've had it with you damn historians," he said, "I want a boat that doesn't rock and makes no waves. Can you do that for me, Ned?"

"Orry really screwed up," was all Hacke could think to say.

"Orry Frank was ambitious, and there's no place in this racket for ambition when it gets out of hand. What I want are selfless people with a sense of loyalty and responsibility. I don't want noise and I don't want a lot of high-flown baloney about the vital mission of the social sciences. I want somebody can keep records and answers his official correspondence and puts a teacher in front of the students in every class who won't generate complaints. Can you do that for me, Ned?"

Ned Hacke lifted his chin, made an effort to set his expression in firm resolve, said, "I'll certainly try with all my heart, Dean Holly." When the word went out on campus, Weber's was the first call he took in his new office, empty since the night Orry Frank packed up and left, musty smelling.

Hacke, having declared his candidacy for the vacant deanship, wondered if he was supposed to campaign for the job. "What," he asked Weber, "do I *do* while I wait around to be interviewed by the search committee?"

"Neddie," Weber told him, "you don't *do* anything. You're not running for election, there's no ballot faculty are going to mark."

"The search committee votes."

"That's a fraud, and you know it, Neddie. You've been playing administrator long enough to know the drill. The Prez designates Gibbs to head up a committee. Jakie handpicks a crew of representative bozos, saps stupid enough to think they're chosen for something important, or else they believe some of Gibbs's power will rub off on them, give them a fine opportunity to osculate the vice-presidential orifice, something they can list in their vita, right? They do the dirty work, screen the outside applications, natter about it, then come up with a short list, which you're already on with the rest of the in-house candidates. You all get phoney-baloney interviews, which Jake Gibbs orchestrates, then Gibbs tells his bozos the three names he prefers to show The Prez, the bozos rubber-stamp same. The Prez I'm assuming asks Gibbs who he's supposed to pick, since Mr. Prez is mostly busy taking trips at the expense of the

Development Foundation or playing golf with regents at the country club, which memberships the Foundation also pays for I hear, providing the weather's good. It's announced over his signature, then we all convene in academic regalia, they hand over the mace of office, presto-chango, you're a dean, Neddie!"

"It's not that simple," Hacke said. "Granting they won't go outside, the others on campus are walking around drumming up support to influence the search committee or Gibbs or both. I should be doing something if I'm serious about this," he said.

"Oh, you're serious, Neddie," Weber said, "which is why you'll fake it you're not because you know it always excites opposition if you look like you want something too much in this game—don't forget Weber's Axiom: the easiest way to make enemies is show ambition, energy, or accomplishment! Besides which, by keeping your profile hunkered down you let the competition go out and demonstrate just how impossible they'd be if they got the job by some cruel twist."

"Or lock it up while I'm pretending I don't care," Hacke said.

"It is but to consider," Weber said, "the nature and quality of your competition, right, Neddie? Feel better already, don't you! I mean, Neddie, your odds get shorter every day!"

"I wonder," Hacke said.

"I don't," Weber said. "Just don't forget who gave you all this keen strategy when you're elevated to a condition of power and greatness, Neddie-boo," he said, "I'm going to expect to be able to take advantage of my friend in a high place, huh?"

"So you're just telling me all this because you want something for it when the time comes?" Hacke said, and smiled.

"Why else would I bother with a dork like you, Neddie?" Weber said, and laughed. Hacke smiled.

Hacke's five months as Head of the History Department terrified him. Because he was the Dean's choice, unsupported by any faction of his faculty, all his colleagues resented him, while, at the same time, each warring group expected him to deliver, to redress long-standing grievances, favor them with special dispensations, and either radically change or preserve forever any feature of the disgraced Orry Frank's administration. Hacke felt trapped, locked in his office, at the mercy of faculty delegations who barged in to demand rights, curry privilege, challenge his least pronouncement, advise or warn him. His only relief was the single course he still taught, but he had already burned out on the classroom experience, so ceased reading the literature of his specialty, lectured from old notes and outlines, lived for five o'clock, when he could flee, go home to a solitary, extended happy hour and an evening of network television.

He had already begun to contemplate resigning—his tenure and promotion slid through as the Dean promised—when he was saved by Dean Holly's structural reorganization of the college.

"What's your opinion of the idea of consolidating departments into school clusters?" he asked Weber.

"I give a rat's ass," Weber said. "What's yours?"

"I'm trying to decide. Sammy Holly's hot for it is all I know."

"Then so are you, Neddie."

"Why?"

"Because," Weber said, "if Sammy wants it, he'll do it regardless of anybody's opinion, so long as Jake and The Prez approved in advance, which they must have, since Mr. Sammy's too smart to even pass gas unless he's greased the chute in advance. You have to figure Holly's got bigger fish to fry somewhere down the line, so he's got to come up with something to create the illusion he's a progressive-thinking educational innovator, right? So he reorganizes the college into a bunch of schools, humanities, social sciences, language and literature, natural and biological sciences, whatever. So what if it creates another layer of bureaucrats, it looks like reform and you're for it."

"Why's that?" Hacke asked.

"Because you eat the Dean's bread, you're the Dean's man, Neddie. Plus there's always a shot you could move up a notch in the shuffle."

Hacke said, "Come off it."

Dean Holly pressed for the reorganization, harangued the faculty at assemblies, browbeat department heads, flooded campus mailboxes with position papers. Hacke got behind it; it gave him time away from the department, closeted with the Dean and his other supporters, and when it came to pass, Sammy Holly tapped Hacke to serve as Director of the School of Social Sciences.

"The moving hand writes," Weber said, "and having writ, moves on. *Up,* huh, Neddie?"

"It's just a title," Hacke said. "Departments retain most budgetary autonomy and there's no salary increment with it."

"Ah, but, Neddie," Weber said, "you're free of teaching responsibilities now—no more classrooms, no more books, no more casting imaginary pearls before real swine!"

"It's not all roses, I'm going to be officed with Schlesinger, Languages and Literature," he said, and, "They say he speaks German more than he does English."

"Uneasy lies the head, Neddie," he said. And he said, "That's a probable plus for you, Neddie. Schlesinger's a notorious world-class dip, you'll look good to Dean Sammy just by contrast."

At first Hacke felt exiled, sharing office space with Schlesinger in an old Quonset left over from a World War II cadet program, drafty, dirty, shabby, and the Director of the School of Languages and Literature was as eccentric as reputed; Dr. Schlesinger addressed him in German more often than in English, behaved erratically, sometimes silent for hours, then suddenly voluble, babbling in German, placing phone calls to his home department. Hacke had almost no real work—he reviewed departmental budgets and personnel actions, calculated enrollment trends, passed correspondence to and from the Dean up or down through the campus mail system, met monthly with the heads of History, Geography, Psychology, and Political Science. So bored he often felt like screaming, at least he received few visitors, taught no students, had no professional obligation to read or write.

Diverting himself with close observation of Dr. Schlesinger, he figured out the problem; the man was seriously alcoholic, and a sweep of the office nooks and crannies while his fellow school director was out one afternoon turned up hidden pints of cut-rate bourbon, the odor of which Schlesinger concealed by chewing raw cloves, the stench of which now permeated their Quonset quarters.

"The man can't have any liver left," he told Weber. "He doesn't *know* he's talking in German is why he does it. I don't know what to do about him, Weber," he said.

"Fink on him," Weber said.

"I'm not that rotten," Hacke said.

"Sure you are, Neddie," Weber said.

He was. Hacke made an appointment with Dean Holly, laid out Schlesinger's situation in detail behind the Dean's closed door. "It's sad, basically," Hacke said. "But I thought you should at least be informed if it wasn't already common gossip on campus." Dean Sammy Holly smiled; he had small, feral teeth. He told Hacke he knew all about Dr. Schlesinger's tippling, said he meant to take action sooner rather than later, had stuck him in that school director's chair to separate him from students, but he greatly appreciated Hacke's coming to him with it.

"I just thought I had a responsibility to at least put you in the picture," Hacke said. Dean Holly put his pale hand on Hack's shoulder as they said goodbye.

"I think, Ned," he said, "you've got the makings of an administrator in you. His department's covered for him for years. You know how faculty stick together. It's nice to find somebody concerned for the college's reputation."

"It was the least I could do," Hacke said.

When he told Weber about it, Weber said, "Score two points for Neddie-boo!" and licked his thumb, made an imaginary mark in the air.

"Guess who dropped in during my office hours yesterday to solicit my support for the deanship," Weber said.

"Potter," Hacke said, imagined the buttoned-down, impeccably groomed biologist breezing into Weber's office, all capped teeth and sprayed coiffure, grinning like a male underwear model, reeking of cologne.

"Guess again."

"Not Ravi," Hacke said; he wouldn't put it past Ravi Singh, who coordinated the International Studies Program, but he'd seen Singh's travel request when it came through the Dean's office, knew he was off campus, in Pakistan or Bangladesh, somewhere, for a conference on current issues in Islamic theology.

"Right," Weber said, "not Sahib Singh."

"I don't believe you," Hacke said. "That leaves Sister Hammer?"

"Give that man a cigar!" Weber said.

"I thought she hated your intestines," Hacke said, shocked.

"Of course she does, and knows it's requited," Weber said, "but she dearly desires Sammy Holly's chair bad enough to swallow her black bile long enough to osculate my orifice, though the subject naturally never came up. Weber's Axiom Number Whatever," he said, "Never put on the agenda the true purpose of any meeting, speak of anything and everything *except* what's at the forefront of everybody's mind, right, Neddie?"

Hacke said, "The dirty bitch!"

Gordon Weaver

"Oh, Neddie," Weber said, "watch out! Your ambition's beginning to show!"

"Do you think she stands the slightest chance?" Hacke asked, unable to prevent the quaver in his voice. Weber laughed until tears filled his eyes. Hacke tried to laugh with him.

Sister Mary Hammer, Ph.D., had been a perfunctory candidate for every administrative opening in the fifteen years since she somehow won tenure in the Psychology Department; to placate her when she lost out each time, she was named to university-wide committees on instructional innovation, core curriculum, roles of women in the profession, academic dishonesty. Sister Mary Hammer was an uncloistered nun constantly at odds with her church's teachings on celibacy, abortion, and the denial of the priesthood to women; her high visibility on campus was the combined result of her bizarre appearance, the doctrinaire Freudian analyses of current political events she published in letters-to-the-editor columns, and the gossip that she was unabashedly lesbian, this last reflected in a stream of poems she had printed at her own expense.

"So what'd you talk about?" Hacke said, and shuddered.

"What else when the good Sapphic seeks my support of her aspirations?" Weber said, and, "Me, of course, Neddie. Sister Mary H. feels very strongly that the university has failed to adequately recognize the excellence of my contribution, and considers, I gather, a regents professorship would be no more than a just recompense for all my considerable accomplishment. I suspect she even may have read my last article to prep herself for the visit!"

"The damn dirty dyke!" Hacke said, then had to laugh again with Weber.

Hacke imagined Sister Mary Hammer as Dean of the College of Arts & Science, saw her bloated, pear-shaped hulk of a body behind Sammy Holly's enormous desk, the dark shadow of her moustache, her waddling gait, the blatantly insincere donkey's bray of her laughter, the camouflage army surplus fatigues and combat boots she wore, envisioned memos couched in Freudian jargon, spun a nightmare fantasy featuring himself, Associate Dean, sitting down knee-to-knee with her for annual performance appraisals, delegating the detail work to him, dependent on her—Hacke felt himself go cold with fear and loathing.

"That's the politics, Neddie. You want to get along, go along. I mean, it works in big city machines, promise them anything for their ballot, dispense the patronage, right?"

"You wouldn't be able to live with yourself with that disgusting pervert for your dean, Weber," he said.

"Oh, I don't know, Neddie me boyo," Weber said, "I sort of fancy myself a regents professor with a reduced teaching load and all that sweetener in my paycheck when I think about it, and," he said, winking, "think how good Gibbs would look with Affirmative Action, a female nun sexual invert heading up one of his colleges?" Hacke tried to laugh, but couldn't until Weber said, "Relax, Neddie! She hasn't got a prayer! *Everybody* hates her as much as you do, even Jake Gibbs. No, Neddie," he said, "Sister Mary ain't your real competition."

"So who is? Ravi? Potter?"

"If I tell you," Weber said, "what will you give me when they turn the purse over to you, Neddie? Would you nominate me for a regents?" Then Hacke could laugh with him, and the cold at the center of him faded away, and he focused his eyes on the wall above Weber's head, set his jaw.

Hacke was the first to know when Bryan Morgan, Holly's associate dean, had his massive coronary. The Dean summoned him early the following morning, told him the news. "Is he going to make it?" Hacke asked.

"Probably. Though it's still touch and go in intensive care,"

Sammy Holly said. "Whatever, Bryan won't be back on the job for months, if ever. I need someone to replace him, Ned. You interested?"

"I'm just getting into the swing of running the school," Hack said while he tried to think what to say, "but if you think I'm right for it, I'm of course ready to come over and fill in until Bryan's back on his feet, if the college needs me." Dean Sammy Holly smiled, revealed his small, sharp teeth; when he smiled, Hacke thought, the Dean looked amazingly like a rat, the teeth, small, close-set eyes, big pointed nose, furtive, nervous hands like forepaws—all he lacked was the twitching whiskers.

"I'll clue you in on the schools, they're going to be abolished," the Dean said.

"I don't get it," Hacke said, "the school system's your big innovation."

"It was," Dean Holly said, "but one of the things you'll learn pretty quicklike up here, Ned," he said, "is flexibility. I made mucho big brownie points with The Prez and Jake Gibbs both with the schools. They like the visibility of moves like that."

"You got a lot of kudos for that," Hacke said, and, "it made sense."

"It did," the Dean said, "but the new thing's going to be biting the budgetary bullet. You been following prognostications for the state's economic situation lately, Ned?"

"It looks grim," Hacke said.

"It *will* be grim. And higher education's going to take our lumps right along with prisons, highways, and the welfare system. At which point the Board of Regents will call on us for sacrifice. At which point The Prez and Gibbs will parrot the call to the university administration, which means no salary increments for faculty this fiscal year."

"They'll kick," Hacke said.

"Let them. Unless we steal their thunder by showing the way with cutting administrative costs."

"The schools," Hacke said.

"You catch on good, Ned," the Dean said. "Are you seeing how many ways it cuts? The faculty's placated because we're giving up school administrators and support staff, sending them back to classroom-teaching Siberia. The Prez and Gibbs applaud because Arts & Science looks so cooperative, as opposed to the other deans who'll scramble to save their sacred turf. Also it gives The Prez big visible cuts to show regents. Which is not to fail to mention how the state legislature is likely to note how *this* college in *this* university showed leadership up front being realistic in a budget crisis year."

"I'm impressed," Hacke said; he was. Then he forced himself to say, "Which also translates," he said, "to no salary increase for yours truly if I take over for Bryan Morgan?"

"Ned!" Dean Holly said. "Would I do that to you? No, we take care of our own children up here!" Sammy Holly said, "Bryan draws his nut out of medical disaster coverage or what's it called, his line item in the budget's freed up, from which I can throw you a bone or six." Dean Holly smiled his rat's smile, and Ned Hacke smiled back at him. "You won't get the same money Bryan got, you don't have that seniority, but you'll feel the difference substantially, to say the least, though," Sammy Holly added, "I'd just as soon you don't spread that for popular consumption on campus, it wouldn't go down well with no raises for faculty when the time comes."

"The budget book's a public document," Hacke said, "they'll go look it up in the library."

"Only the soreheads like your pal Weber," Dean Holly said, "and nobody gives a crap what he thinks about anything anyhow." And the Dean laughed, showed his teeth, and Hacke laughed.

Weber was the first to call him when the word went out on campus. "Congrats, Neddie," he said, "I hear Morgan's on indefinite medical leave if he doesn't actually croak, so you're in like Flynn, huh?"

"I'm only Acting Interim Associate," he said.

"What are your duties?" Weber asked. "I mean, in addition to wiping off Holly's shaft for him when he pulls it out of the faculty."

"You're a hopeless cynic, Weber," he said. "I've got the college budget primarily, personnel, everything except research and extension service. It's a big job," he said.

"That should leave Sammy free to politic," Weber said. "Calls for a big salary, Neddie."

"Nobody's getting raises this fiscal year, Weber," Hacke said. "Haven't you been following the state's economy? It's bullet-biting time, Weber."

"I'll believe that when I see it in the budget book in the library come fall semester, Neddie," Weber said.

"You know what your trouble is?" he told him. "You're a sorehead. No wonder nobody takes you seriously for all your professional distinction, Weber." Weber exploded with laughter on the telephone, and Hacke pretended to laugh with him.

"Tell me, Neddie-boo," Weber said when he stopped laughing, "is it true you can actually *feel* the energy Sammy gives off, officed right next to him over there? Does he really have that sort of radioactive aura glowing around him when you're up close, like I've heard? Tell me what that hundred-and-ten-pound little nerve-end's *really* like, Neddie!"

"He's a man going places," Hacke said.

Weber said, "I better let you go so you can get you a good grip on his coattails, Neddie. Hey, did you ever notice how much Sammy-boy looks for all the world like some kind of rodent?"

"No," Hacke said, and, "I've got work to do."

"Liar!" Weber said, still laughing when Hacke hung up on him.

"Granted," Hacke said to Weber, "Sister Hammer's out of the running, I don't see how you discount Singh so glibly."

"Neddie," Weber said, "your vision's clouded. The tension's starting to get to you, or else you've been cheek-to-jowl with Holly so long you've stopped looking, all you see is what you want to."

"He's got some reputation," Hacke said. "He's always hauling off to give speeches about Islamic religion."

"True."

"He runs his shop over there okay," Hacke said, "we've got more international enrollment paying out-of-state tuition rates than ever before, he gets donations from Saudis and Libya, he's got ties with Vietnamese refugee organizations are going to get him federal funds for language instruction."

"True."

"He's as devious as Gibbs or even The Prez," Hacke said, "he's got all the traits you need to be dean."

"True," Weber said.

"So where do you get off discounting him the same way you do our fat dyke nun candidate?"

"Oh, Neddie," Weber said, "have you forgotten this is, after all, America?" Weber explained it to him, convinced him Dr. Ravi Singh, Director of International Studies, coordinator of the international student recruitment program, was no real competition for Sammy Holly's chair.

Granted, Ravi Singh had some reputation, flew across the country, overseas, to make presentations about the current state of missionary Islam; Ravi Singh ran his shop efficiently, boasted massive increases in enrollments from the Third World, had his finger on grant monies put up by some OPEC countries; it went without saying, Ravi Singh was consistently conspiratorial, could be counted on to prevaricate in any context when it served him or any administrative superior. All this meant, Weber said, was that Dr. Ravi Singh was as good a name as Sister Hammer's to put on the recruiting report Jake Gibbs was required by law to submit to Affirmative Action once the search for the new dean was history.

"You're illogical," Hacke said.

"Neddie," Weber said, "consider: Sahib Singh's complexion is approximately the shade of imported Dutch chocolate—is The Prez going to have a dean he wouldn't invite to a regents' cocktail party? Sahib Singh speaks an English about on a par with that guru used to be on television, the one talked Transcendental Meditation to all the celebrities—you think Jakie Gibbs is going to sit by in his cap and gown at Arts & Science Convocation every autumn and listen to an address half the audience can't understand? He's the wrong hue, he talks like Gunga Din, his idea of formal attire is a bush jacket and open-toe sandals, he has a degree from *India,* Neddie! He writes articles praising Khaddaffi!"

"You're a bigot," Hacke said.

"No," Weber said, "I'm not, but The Prez is, and so's Gibbs if he thinks he should be, and so's half our faculty and three-fourths of our student body, and probably 90 percent of the regents—where the hell you think you are, Neddie, Ivy League?"

"Okay," Hacke said, "so there's no threat from Ravi," he said, "that leaves Potter."

"Give the man ten silver dollars!" Weber said. "Now you're cooking. Richie Potter's your rival, Neddie-boy!"

"I'm dead in the water," Hacke said.

"Probably not," Weber said, and explained to him why he

thought Hacke was the odds-on favorite to get Dean Holly's vacated chair.

Being Sammy Holly's Acting Interim Associate Dean was a bigger job than Hacke expected. What it meant was doing Holly's work, because Dean Holly was busy, at work with the leading candidate for governor in the next election, writing his position papers on public education. "If he wins," Hacke asked, "are you going with his team to the state house?"

"Time will tell, Ned," Sammy Holly said, and smiled his rodent's smile, rubbed his frisking hands.

Hacke made the budget balance, reviewed the hirings and firings and tenure recommendations that came up from academic departments, monitored the college's advisory committees, sitting in ex-officio for the Dean. He authored the Dean's memos, told departments yea or nay in Sammy Holly's name, responded to Vice-President Gibbs's requests; inside a month on the job, faculty and staff figured out Hacke was the man to seek appointments with—Dean Holly was busy with more pressing matters; his gubernatorial candidate showed seemingly invincible strength in all the polls.

Hacke discovered he had a style that worked. His wardrobe —nondescript three-piece suits, plain ties, sensible shoes—was right to begin with. He got his hair sculptor-cut more frequently, took care of his fingernails, clipped the stubble that protruded from his nostrils. He invested in an expensive fountain pen.

He choreographed his office decor. His desk was only a little smaller than the Dean's, and he kept it cleared, paperwork stacked in lucite tiers on the credenza behind his huge swivel chair, the surface polished with a lemon scent each morning by his personal secretary before he showed up for work. On the built-in bookshelves, he instructed her to keep the bound volumes of college reports, catalogues, policy and procedure manuals, and university yearbooks dusted, lined up like soldiers in ranks.

He hung lithographs of the Parthenon, the Acropolis, and Rome's amphitheater on his walls, bought three plaster replicas of classical statuary to sit on his broad windowsills, placed two large books containing color plates of ancient art on the coffee table. When he had a visitor, he always had him or her announced on his intercom, always made the appointment wait for two to six minutes before he buzzed his secretary to tell her to show Professor Whoever in. When Professor Whoever entered his office, Hacke was always sitting back, huddled, in his chair, but always rose, came out from behind his desk, shook hands even if he'd seen the professor half an hour earlier, sat beside him or her on the sofa at the coffee table.

Hacke learned a listening pose, to squint as if concentrating, to look into his visitor's eyes without seeing him or her, to respond laconically in a barely audible voice, never to answer in the end except to say he'd get back to the professor as soon as possible. When he wrote informal notes in response to correspondence, he contrived a very tiny script, signed with his initials, never his full name. His secretary responded to all phone calls with the information that Dr. Hacke was in conference, took a number for call-back.

"Oh, Neddie, oh, Neddie!" Weber said when he came to see him there, had to dry his eyes on his handkerchief when he at last choked off his laughter. Hacke refused to laugh with him, would not permit himself even to smile.

"You want a cup of coffee? My secretary keeps the brewer in her office, I'll give her a buzz if you want some," he said to Weber.

"Neddie," Weber said, "I begin to seriously think you're

going to be a force to be reckoned with. Hey," he said, "I hope I didn't disturb the Dean with my laughing, that door connects to his sanctum if I'm not mistaken."

"He's off campus," Hacke said, "at some sort of political confab with our next governor. Is this social," Hacke said, "or did you have some business for me?"

Hacke said, "It's Potter, it's going to be Potter, I can feel it in my bones. They drag me up here to do Bryan Morgan's job, I'm doing Holly's work even before he runs off to suck up with that crooked son of a bitch we elected governor of the state, then drop me like a bad habit and give the chair to slick weasel Richie Potter!"

"Possibly," Weber said, "except for the fact I can see where Richie isn't all that right for the deanship, Neddie."

"What the hell kind of a system leads a man on up the path and then dumps on him!" Hacke said.

"Your kind, Neddie," Weber said.

"Go ahead, gloat," he said when Weber got to laughing.

Richie Potter, Hacke believed, was going to be the new dean of the college. It was obvious, a cinch. Jake Gibbs was going to convene his phoney-baloney search committee, they'd toss out the off-campus candidates, then hold interviews; they'd trot Hacke, the fat dyke nun, and Sahib Ravi Singh past them, then give Richie Potter an audience, adjourn for the pretense of deliberation and voting, and then The Prez would announce what was fixed from the start: Sammy Holly's successor was Dr. Richie Potter, Professor of Physics.

Hacke said, "The nasty bastard *looks* like a damn dean!"

Professor Richie Potter was strikingly handsome, tall and trim; he wore his prematurely snow white hair almost shoulder length, styled in waves and falls like a heap of caterer's meringue; Richie Potter was permanently tanned, looked like a man who surfed or climbed mountains, the result of regular hours under a lamp; when he walked across campus, Richie Potter *strode,* his gait a bouncy springing suggesting he barely contained his unflagging energies; Richie Potter's even teeth gleamed when he smiled, and he always smiled; his wardrobe was color coordinated, but not sporty or ostentatious; his voice was deep and clear, audible in every corner of any room without benefit of amplification; when he signed off on a memo, Richie Potter's hand was bold, symmetrical, half again as large as any normal holograph; Richie Potter had a wife who, though in open violation of the state's nepotism statute, had her own following in the computer science lab; their children were Merit Scholars!

"I'd say Richie-poo looks almost presidential, which is scary considering how The Prez will reach mandatory retirement in but a few short years," Weber said, gagging on his laugh.

"Thanks," Hacke said, and, "Why don't you tell me how great his research is while you're at it giving me the needle, Weber!"

"I would," Weber cackled, "but it's common knowledge all over campus, Neddie!"

Hacke believed: the new dean was going to be Dr. Richie Potter! Richie Potter had a national reputation, flew in and out of Washington like a commuter to maintain his National Science Foundation contacts, received astronomical grants from the Department of Defense for continued applied research in remote sensing, directly relevant to the space program, Star Wars—Professor Richie Potter had it all, surface and substance, and he was going to get the job Ned Hacke had almost come to think was his, *should* be his!

"I feel snake-bit," Hacke said.

"You're forgetting, Neddie," Weber said.

"Forgetting what?"

"The fact," Weber said, "that his impressive record, not to

mention his tangible abilities, with the added advantage of his sterling personality and fashion-plate image, are a distinct liability for the deanship, Neddie."

"What the hell are you talking about? Are you enjoying rubbing my face in it, Weber?" he asked.

"Neddie," Weber said, "not to despair, Neddie-boo! I mean, here you are, totally unfit for it, and just look how far you've come so far, Neddie!" Hacke laughed with him, if only to keep from weeping.

His interview with the search committee was exactly what Hacke dreaded; the fix was in! He went through the experience like a sleepwalker, as if it were a bad dream, a semisurreal drama that epitomized all the sham and fraud at the heart of academic life.

Hacke was the third of the four on-campus candidates interviewed on successive afternoons. On Monday and Tuesday, Vice-President Gibbs and his four stooges went through the motions with Sister Mary Hammer and Ravi Singh—they saved Richie Potter for last, a blatant ploy, Hacke understood, to conceal the precedence they'd already granted him—it was rigged all the way! Hacke nearly pulled his application the morning of the day of his interview, would have if Weber hadn't insisted he swallow the shreds of his pride and let them play out their dirty game with him.

"You can't do any worse than our dyke nun or Sahib Ravi," Weber said.

"Why subject myself to it?" Hacke said, "It's Potter, and I'm just one more loser they can humiliate when The Prez announces it."

"Aren't you hearing campus rumors, Neddie?" Weber asked. "Sister Hammer went on for an hour about some center for female studies alternative life-styles institute she'll establish when she takes the chair. Sahib Singh didn't have anything to say except about the financial importance of recruiting more foreign students to pay out-of-state tuition rates, besides which he spoke so fast the committee couldn't understand half of it. Richie-boy's going to grin at them and cut poses and brag about all his N.S.F. funding—what have you got to lose, Neddie?"

"So what am I supposed to talk about if they ask me for my ideas for the college's future?" he said.

"Exactly what they want to hear," Weber said. "Nothing. Generalities. Bromides. Stock phrases. The pieties of the mission of higher education as we confront the next century, etcetera blah, blah!"

"Oh," Hacke said, "I'll be just simply fascinating!"

"It's what you're good at, Neddie," Weber said.

So Dr. Ned Hacke was on time for his interview; the only satisfaction he took in the ordeal was the blatant corroboration of his suspicions.

Jake Gibbs presided, said, "Everybody knows Professor Hacke, and we've all studied his vita along with the other candidates, so I think we can just proceed casually. I'll turn it over to my distinguished committee colleagues to conduct our discussion here, reserving the option to chime in if something of particular interest to me chances to come up." But he never did. The Vice-President for Academic Affairs sat silent throughout the fifty minutes of Hacke's interview, a distracted half-smile on his face; Hacke wondered if Gibbs had turned off his hearing aid.

"Professor Hacke," Paul Klemperer said, "I'd like to have you talk about *why* you want to be a dean."

"I see the deanship," Hacke said, "as an opportunity to bring my ability and my energy and my vision—if that's not too pompous a term—to the service of my college and this university, a wider arena, if you will, for the same service I've tried to render through administration since I began initially not so long ago as a department head." Klemperer was clearly a Potter supporter; representing the physical sciences faculty, Potter's home shop, he'd even done some work with Potter on remote sensing—Hacke couldn't bear to look at Klemperer's face as he spoke, so fixed on the physicist's hands, watched him make what must have been verbatim notes of everything Hacke said. He looked up whenever Klemperer spoke, flinched when he made contact, the man's thick glasses magnifying and distorting his pin-hole eyes. Klemperer, Hacke thought: one sure vote for Richie Potter.

"Dr. Hacke," Professor Ossie Bruce said, "what would you say are the most important things you've accomplished as an administrative officer at this university to date?"

"I consider my contribution," Hacke said, "to be primarily one of maintaining and enhancing the stability of whatever unit I've served. It seems to me *stability* is something we often overlook which is vital to the professional lives of all our colleagues." Ossie Bruce, Professor of Biology, notorious administrative toady, representing life sciences faculty, was another Potter vote—the sciences always went for one of their own, had no respect for anyone outside their ranks, smug in the conviction of the material utility of their disciplines, fat on government grant money, aloof from what they thought of as the frills of education—the *soft* disciplines, they called them. Ossie Bruce, whose work involved breeding an organism that could eat petroleum, thus clean up oil spills, listened to Hacke with a frozen sneer of scientist's skepticism on his face. Two votes for Potter, the good old boy network of science!

"Would you care to give us your definition of *liberal* education?" Professor Elizabeth Terwilliger asked him. She represented humanities. Commonly called *Eliza-bitch* by her colleagues in English, she was often mistaken, at a distance, for a man. She was given to wearing slacks and blazers with padded shoulders, her hair cut short and shaved on her nape, and Hacke could discern no slightest trace of breasts poking from either side of the regimental necktie she wore. He didn't think she was a dyke, just androgynous—she would naturally vote for Sister Hammer.

"*Liberal,*" Hacke said, "is one of those troublesome buzz-words we labor under in our profession. I don't think its defini-tion is so important so much as it's important we strive to keep *evolving* a definition we can live with." Eliza-bitch: one vote for Sister Hammer.

"What's your opinion of the biggest challenge we face in Arts & Science in the next few years, Professor Hacke?" Dr. Zora Coleman asked him.

"Challenge," Hacke said, "is inherent in the tripartite mission of education, research, and service." Zora Coleman had been a hot property when she was hired in sociology, a black female with relatively respectable credentials, but a disappointment since. Named, for her race, to every ad hoc committee—it was called *spreading the black around*—she'd abandoned her research for a career as perpetual minority token to keep Affirmative Action off the university's back. Representing social sciences on the search committee, she should have leaned toward Hacke, but he knew she'd either vote for Singh on the basis of shared color, or join forces with Eliza-bitch Terwilliger in favor of Sister Ham-mer, however confusing the gender factor might be.

For fifty minutes, Jake Gibbs sat as if he were alone in the room, communing with his immortal soul or snoozing; his four stooges delivered their rehearsed, pontifical queries; Hacke re-gurgitated the commonplaces they'd all been hearing all their adult lives. It ran down to an awkward silence, and then the Vice-President seemed to wake suddenly, as if jarred by an epiphany, said, "I think we've all heard what we came for," and the session adjourned.

"How'd it go, Neddie?" Weber phoned to ask.

"I'd rather have a root canal," he told him, and, "It was scripted all the way. The sciences go with Richie Potter, Eliza-bitch pushes our nun dyke, Ruby Begonia recommends Ravi because we don't do enough for our darker brethren—I wish I was old enough to take early retirement," he said.

"Now, Neddie-poo," Weber said, "hold your water! It ain't over till The Prez pronounces, right?"

Dr. Ned Hacke, Associate Professor of History, was installed in the office of Dean of the College of Arts & Science at a formal ceremony of investiture staged in the university's student union grand ballroom. The extraordinary convocation was called by The Prez, who presided. In attendance were Vice-President for Academic Affairs Jake Gibbs, the vice-presidents for university finance, student affairs, and extension services, the deans of the colleges of business administration, education, veterinary med-icine, home economics, and engineering studies, the faculty of Arts & Science, and even a scattering of students, all but the last attired in full academic regalia. The former Dean, Sammy Holly, state superintendent-designate of public education, was present to represent the governor's office, as was the executive secretary of the Board of Regents, a man who owned a meat-packing corporation.

The relatively simple ritual, devised by a member of the Theater Department, began with the procession of administra-tive officers down a center aisle to the dais, to the accompani-ment of the strains of *Pomp and Circumstance* and the applause of the standing audience. The dais party seated, the music ceased, and The Prez invited the audience to sit also, following this with a short peroration, written by his secretary, invoking the tradition of the university and the college, the various crises facing higher education, with their attendant opportunities for excellence, and the solemnity of the present instance, concluding with fulsome praise of the university's faculty and the new dean they had assembled to honor and install in office.

Hacke, seated just to one side of the podium where The Prez held forth, took the occasion to consider his triumph. It had, Jake Gibbs confided as the word went out on campus, never been in doubt; candidates from outside were always a questionable commodity; Sister Mary Hammer and Ravi Singh were recognized at once as quite impossible—the former a grotesque embarrassment, the latter an energetic man, but his English was simply unintelligible to most native speakers, and was one to appoint a dean who might show up at a meeting with regents wearing a turban? Both were, however, a credit to the recruiting report submitted to Affirmative Action, and both would be tossed bones of consolation, perhaps some limited funding for feminist studies until that craze died of its own inertia, a bit more visibility for Islamic scholarship and Professor Singh. Richie Potter was simply too valuable to the university to move from research to administration; it was inconceivable to give up a pipeline to National Science Foundation dollars—a regents professorship was in order for Dr. Potter.

When Hacke was bold enough to ask the Vice-President what virtues they saw in him, Gibbs cited his administrative experience and the strong confidence both he and The Prez felt in him: Ned Hacke was no rocker of boats, no maker of waves, they *knew* they could count on him to raise no dust, to maintain and enhance the college's stability within the university family of colleges, as Hacke, Gibbs noted, had put it so eloquently during his interview.

And Hacke *would,* he vowed as The Prez finished his remarks. He, Hacke, would run his shop, hold fast to the tiller that was the dean's chair, guide this ship that was his college through the straits, over the shoals, around the rapids of difficulty and complexity as they approached them in these trying, challenging days to come!

When Hacke stood to receive the dean's mace of office from The Prez, the tassel of the mortarboard dangling before his nose, he looked out at the clapping audience, again on its feet, caught Sammy Holly's rat-smile of approval, located Weber, his face convulsed, shoulders under his gown shaking with laughter. He gripped the heavy mace, almost as tall as he was, in both hands, followed after The Prez as the recessional progress began.

He walked slowly, careful not to trod on The Prez's heels, the mace's bulk and weight awkward, passed down the ballroom aisle, flicking glances at his colleagues. Sister Mary Hammer, enormous under the tent of her academic robe, looked as if she suffered nauseating cramps; Ravi Singh would not look at him, seemed lost, as if immersed in some mystic trance-state. Richie Potter flashed his omnipresently insincere grin of camaraderie. He passed Paul Klemperer, Ossie Bruce, Eliza-bitch Terwilliger, Zora Coleman, clapping in perfect unison.

When he passed near Weber, the man winked at him, leaned out from his row, shouted through the applause, "Don't drop it, Neddie, it could damage your manhood!"

Hacke looked away, held the tighter to the mace of his new office. He concentrated on the back of The Prez's neck—the old man was only a bit taller than Hacke; he was surprised to see how frail he looked at such close range, his wispy white hair hanging in tatters from under his mortarboard, his slumped posture, tedious, faltering steps—yes, Hacke thought, The Prez was getting on, would have to retire sooner rather than later. Who was to say who might succeed him?

Dean Hacke held that thought, something to look to down the road; more immediately, his first task in office was going to be to straighten Professor Weber out. Dr. Weber, Dean Ned

Hacke thought, was going to have to change his tune if he wanted to get along with the man in the dean's chair now! Let him, Hacke thought, call me *Neddie* just once!

Pomp and Circumstance still playing, the Dean lifted his chin, allowed himself the trace of a smile, as, behind him in the ballroom, the applause slowed, faded, and died.

BATTEIGER'S MUSE

 C♦Ɔ

My tongue is the pen of a ready writer.
—Book of Common Prayer

His Muse came to him in the morning, as Batteiger sat at his writing table. Elbows flanking a blank legal pad, chin in his hands, Batteiger stared at the empty yellow page, sharpened Number 2 Ticonderoga lying diagonally across his line of sight, Camel burning in the heaped ashtray, coffee cooling in a chipped mug. Batteiger, mired for months in a monumental Block, was torn: pick up the pencil, write the first word of the first sentence of a novel flitting just beyond the reach of his sterile imagination or sweep the table's surface clear, put his head down, and weep.

He heard a popping sound, like a cork drawn, looked up, and there she was—his Muse—floating in midair just inside his apartment window. There was a dull glow to her, a fuzzy shimmering. She sat in the middle of this uncertain aura, as if sprawled on a sofa or chaise longue, shoulders back, legs indecorously apart, something between a coy smile and a leer on her fat face. She was no more than six inches tall. When she spoke, the normal volume of her voice came to him through a keen ringing in his ears.

Batteiger's Muse said, "What's happening, Batteiger? How they hanging?" And she winked obscenely.

When he could speak, Batteiger said, "I won't let myself believe this."

She said, "Nice stinking welcome, Batteiger! Come all this way to pull your stones out of the crack, set you straight, that's all you got to say? Come off it, Batteiger," she said, "you know you been waiting on me to show, right? And quit sneaking a peek up my dress," she said, tugging down her skirt.

When he could speak again, Batteiger said, "I need to start drinking a better label."

She laughed a big, throaty, raucous laugh, as if he'd told a nasty joke, leaned forward to expose the chasm of her cleavage. "Get real. I'm your Muse, Batteiger," Batteiger's Muse said.

"This is *not* happening to me!" Batteiger said.

"Can we get on with it?" she said, paused to bite at her cuticle, spit the flake of skin on his desk below where she hovered; Batteiger watched it fall, land on his legal pad.

"You're the Muse?"

"*Your* Muse," Batteiger's Muse said. "Maybe you should wash the wax out of your ears so's I don't got to chew my words only once, huh?"

Once upon a time, when Batteiger was an adolescent who wrote erotic lyrics about girls who didn't even know his name, he imagined a Muse, mostly modeled on classical references, jazzed up to look sort of contemporary. He raged with dry lust after indifferent schoolgirls, poems poured out of him like lava, and his Muse took the shapes, in turn, of various Hollywood starlets, but each had wings and wore a peek-a-boo toga, spoke in rhymes tight as Pope's couplets.

In college, he dreamed about her once; she looked very like his composition instructor, a busty spinster named Bea who gave him a B, but told him he had talent—he lacked only discipline and any knowledge of grammar or punctuation.

When a nonpaying quarterly took his first story, a tale of an adolescent poet seduced by a nymphomaniacal English teacher, Batteiger envisioned a Muse who wore a low-cut evening gown, her red hair in a sleek chignon, lips colored like fresh blood, long nails to match, a miasma of Shalimar enveloping her, an editor's blue pencil she tapped against her ivory teeth as she read his work-in-progress. And wings. Smaller, folded out of sight until she spread them to soar with him.

When he sold his first novel, over the transom, a *Bildungs-roman* that alienated his parents and siblings, but got a semi-rave *Times* review, Batteiger caught a last glimpse of her: pretty much the same, except her makeup was subdued, perfume muted, the wings forgotten. He got an agent—Nate Schimpf. His second novel brought a big advance. But the book, a very long narrative about a first novelist's struggle to repeat on the best-seller list, was so dramatic a failure—no major reviews, remaindered within the year—he wised up in a hurry.

Fed up, his wife divorced him and remarried, removed their daughter with her to California, refused to allow him visits until he paid up the child support in arrears. The new novel, now a projected epic exploration of the disastrous course of a modern marriage, dried up like spit on a sidewalk. Batteiger hadn't thought about the Muse for half a decade, and Nate Schimpf no longer returned his calls.

"You don't look like the Muse," Batteiger said.

"*Your* Muse. I already told you. And you don't hardly look like no picture of no big writer neither," she said. His ears rang, and she pulsed within her aura.

"Am I seeing things or are you getting bigger as I'm looking?" he asked.

"A hair's worth I think," she said. "Watch," she said, "the

more you cotton to the general idea, I'll get full-size I'd guess. You like largish big-bone women, Batteiger?"

"Where's your wings?" Batteiger said. She laughed so hard she began to cough, a hoarse smoker's hack.

She was a big, porky woman, all . . . what, eight inches of her now? Her stringy hair looked dirty, uncombed. Her skin was bad, dark circles under her piggy, glassy eyes. Her soiled blouse was unbuttoned one button too many—her puffy breasts were mottled with freckles and moles. She had a spare tire, and her haunches and bulbous thighs spread like pillows under her wrinkled skirt. She had a scab on one knee, stubble on her thick legs. Dingy socks drooped over her scuffed, mannish shoes. Through the screech in his ears, her fluid aura, he smelled a whiff of body odor.

"To begin," Batteiger said, "you could probably use a bath."

"Don't let's get personal. And name the last time you changed your shorts, Batteiger," Batteiger's Muse said.

"What Muse bites her fingernails?"

"*Yours!* What big writer-type don't shave regular and uses the same snotrag for days?"

"You could dress to better advantage."

"I guarantee you," she said, "you'll be really bald soon. I can spot male-pattern a mile away."

"Nor are you especially articulate."

"Oh," Batteiger's Muse said, "listen to the hotshot wordsmith, will you? Which is why," she said, "you're so blocked you're constipated. Which is why," she said, "you ain't made a dent even in that crappy novel you think you're writing, which is why your agent give up on you, plus which your ex's about to garnishee what little pot you got left to pee in, plus which your kid don't even remember what her old man looks like if she met him on the street, plus which—"

"Give me a damn break!" Batteiger shouted. His Muse flickered, faded an instant, reformed like congealing oil.

"Why else," she said, "you think I'm here, Batteiger?"

He closed his eyes, opened them, and she was gone. The view from his window was, again, his view—the street, passing vehicles, a pair of cyclists, a lone pedestrian. There was no ringing in his ears.

He believed it was some sort of hysteria, some jolt in his brain, maybe chemical, a conscious fantasy. Anything was possible, Batteiger thought—until he looked down at his legal pad, spotted the tiny shred of skin, smaller than a flea, lying beside his Ticonderoga; he stabbed it with the sharpened point, lifted it up into the window's light, a translucent dot that shone like foil. He shuddered, broke the pencil in two, took the day off—no way Batteiger was going to be able to write anything that day!

By the time his mail was delivered, he was thinking only sporadically about her, smiling to himself, even wondering if there was a story somewhere in it he might write once he got the novel's momentum rolling. The day's mail included a letter from his daughter, folded inside one from his ex-wife, and a note from Nate Schimpf.

Nate scrawled under his letterhead:

Sorry to be so long getting back to you—busy busy busy!!—nothing to report here—call from publ. the other day asking about W.I.P. What do I tell them? How about you give me first chapt. w/outline? Keep touch.
Best,
Nate

Batteiger's ex-wife typed:

I agreed to enclose this only because I continue to hope there is still some hope you will meet your obligation. Do not reply unless and until you are prepared to remit that which a court order ordered. I will also remind you there are legal procedures available at my discretion to me. This is not an idle threat. Doubtless you are content to play the author starving in his attic garret. I am professionally advised this line of argument will not prevail with civil authority.

It was unsigned. His daughter block-printed:

Dear Dad,
    How are you? I am fine. Will you come to visit me soon? I like California. It never rains if you play outside. My new dad is nice. I hope you are fine. I am very fine. We have a new dog pet.
    Your child Grace B.

To avoid total collapse, Batteiger started drinking earlier than usual that afternoon. He passed out on his Murphy bed, woke at dawn, stricken with a triple-A, certified hangover, shuffled to the bathroom, dry-heaved, drank cold water from the faucet, splashed his face, looked at his ravaged image in the cabinet mirror. "Today," Batteiger said solemnly, voice a croak, "I *will* begin my novel."

"In a pig's ass!" Batteiger's Muse said to him. The faint pop was barely discernible, simultaneous with her words; the noise in his ears this time was only a gentle hum. As he looked into the mirror, she seemed to be perched on his shoulder, her aura faded to a kind of subtle backlighting. She sat cross-legged, coyly bobbing her foot; the smell of her was stronger, as if they embraced.

"Oh God oh Lord God," Batteiger said, reached back to touch her, knock her off his shoulder—watching in the mirror, he saw his hand pass through her, withdrew it as it he'd been bitten when he felt the sudden warmth in his fingers.

"Trying to cop a feelie, Batteiger?" his Muse said, pouted, shook her finger. "Naughty, naughty!" she said. "Polite persons ask permission first!" When he closed and opened his eyes, she was still there. She was a good foot and a half tall now.

Batteiger's Muse

Batteiger's Muse said, "Cut the crapola, OK? You're up the crick, you interested in maybe a paddle?" He shut his eyes, braced his hands against the mirror, willed her away, but she kept talking.

"Face it, Batteiger. Why's Nate even bother to write a so-called writer who owes a biggie advance on a novel ain't been written, ain't *going* to get written by you! Think maybe your publisher's thinking maybe time to call in the advance? And the ex did you a number I'd say—has little Grace twist your sack some, harps on lawyer's advice to garnishee you. Hoo-boy!" his Muse shouted. "Have they got you by the short ones or what, Batteiger!"

Eyes squeezed shut, he felt his way out of the bathroom, stumbled through the hall past the kitchen, groped around his Murphy bed, sat at his writing table before opening his eyes. She sat, legs tucked under her, amid his rumpled sheets; she looked to have grown another half-foot. "I give up," Batteiger said.

"Aw, Batteiger," his Muse said, batted her pale lashes at him, thrust out her pimpled chin, "don't be so easy! I mean, a gal likes to enjoy working up to it a little, right?" She laughed her vulgar laugh, said, "So, ready to listen, are we, Mr. Big Writer Batteiger?"

"I feel stupid," Batteiger said. "What's your name?"

"Alma Jean. Like it?"

"It's a hell of a name for a Muse."

"*Your* Muse. What'd you expect, *Calliope,* for the shit's sakes?"

"Where'd you come from? Do you live someplace when you're not here?"

"Not hardly. I been with you since you started scribbling, you just wouldn't admit."

"I'm, like, imagining you?"

"Sort of. Don't futz up your head asking questions from a gift horse, Batteiger."

"And you can inspire me?"

"I can do better than that, honey!" she said, licking her lips.

"Help me with the novel?" he said.

"Novel schmovel," she said. "What you need is cash flow, right?"

"So you'll set it up for me to inherit money or find a crock of gold, like that?"

She tipped her head back, kicked her feet, laughed long and hard, wheezing. "Hey, you're a *writer*! What I do is, I find you paying work for your talents, OK?"

"Such as?"

"*Literary* work, what else? Hey," she patted the bed with her palm, "come sit closer so's we can talk better, huh?"

"I'd rather not," Batteiger said, smelling her.

"Hard to get," said his Muse. "I dig a guy makes me a challenge, Batteiger!" And she laughed, and he tried to laugh with her.

Out of the blue, Batteiger got paying work suitable to his talents. The arts and entertainment editor of the city's major daily called, asked him to do an omnibus review-essay of half a dozen first novels getting a lot of prepublication attention; the books were delivered by messenger, Batteiger skimmed them, knocked out two thousand words—thin summary and sheer pontification—in an afternoon. The piece, under his byline in boldface, held the Sunday supplement's center, and his check for five hundred big ones came by messenger the next day, with a note from the editor telling him it was great stuff, was he interested in regular reviewing, a books column?

The day after that, Batteiger's mail brought a commission from a national magazine, one of the quasi-intellectual slick monthlies, for an article on the current literary scene; the contract called for two thou, with a seven hundred fifty dollar kill-fee if it failed to run, two-fifty up front when he signed on the dotted line. He signed, spent a day at the public library check-ing out a month's reviews, took notes he rephrased to avoid plagiarism, whacked out five thousand words in two days. The magazine snapped it up the day after he submitted the manu-script, a check for the balance of his commission in the next mail. It ran in the next issue, with a bio blurb calling Batteiger a *writer-critic*.

While he waited for the article to appear, he got a query from a job publisher in the Midwest asking him if he was interested in freelance editing—they had an eighteen-hundred-page tele-communications management manual that needed going over. In a handwritten postscript, the editorial director said the per-page rate for a man of Batteiger's facility should work out to an easy hundred dollars an hour. He wavered, but the bucks were too tempting; when he set to on the job, he was surprised how effortless it felt, that he rather enjoyed rearranging structure, imposing a neutrally formal style on the material, playing with punctuation. The editorial director had not said where he got Batteiger's name from.

His Muse never showed.

Batteiger wrote his ex-wife a polite letter, enclosed a tenderly warm holograph to his daughter, along with a money order for three hundred dollars to prove the integrity of his intentions.

Nate Schimpf telephoned, said, "Batteiger? I been neglecting you, tell me about it! Loved your piece on the lit scene, by the way! That's the old Batteiger prose I always knew you got in you. Reason I called, on the off-chance you can steal a little time away from the opus, I'm in contact with a guy was in on the absolute inside of some of these big stock scandal deals? He's looking for a ghost to write it up for him in a hurry, he's already got the biggest houses in Gotham salivating for it, get me?"

"You want me to ghostwrite a book about the stock market?" Batteiger said.

"I'm talking twenty K openers, nice cut from royalty and subsidiaries, and I know you can do this left-handed and still chip away at the tome, Batteiger. What say, interested?"

Instead of refusing it, he said, "Let me ponder a while, Nate."

"Don't do me no big favors just because I wrangled you a huge advance you're not delivering on, Batteiger," his agent said.

"I'm not saying no," Batteiger said. "I'll get back to you to-morrow, OK?" When he hung up, stood staring down at his phone, he swore he heard Alma Jean's laughter, if only for a moment, as if she were out in the kitchen.

Batteiger's Muse was waiting for him the next morning, sit-ting in his kitchen when he got up to make coffee. She'd already brewed it, sat with a cup in front of her, smoking one of his Camels, dressed in a rumpled bathrobe, feet bare, as if she'd slept the night somewhere in his apartment. Her hair un-combed, eyes still smudged a little from sleep, she laughed and grinned when he gaped at her, showed her stained teeth. She was at least five feet tall, smelled like his Murphy bed.

"There's my big writer man!" she said. "Cat got your tongue, sweets? Have a cup of coffee before you call Nate, why don't you, love?"

"OK, so you know everything," Batteiger said to his Muse.

"And then some, doll-boy," she said, laughed. "Now," she said, "sit down, drink your coffee"—she shook a Camel from his pack for him—"it's time we let it all hang out, if you'll pardon my French."

"I'm telling Nate to pass on me for that ghosting thing." She lit his cigarette for him, let her free hand cover his as she held the match up; a hot flash ran through him. "I've got some breathing room now, I need to get back on the novel."

"Yeah," Alma Jean said. "Sure thing. And I got to practice my piano for the Miss America, too."

"I'm a writer. I write. I'm a serious writer, I write serious literary novels," he said. "I don't ghost *schlock*. "Go away. Dematerialize. I don't need you."

"Like you didn't need the big book review in the Sunday paper paid you five yards. Like you don't need articles in big-time slickie mags pay kill-fees millions of people read. Like you don't need twenty K up front from Nate's stockbroker thief guy, plus not to mention a movie sale and probably translations. Like you don't need the scratch to mail your ex so little Gracie don't forget her real daddy," Alma Jean said.

"That's all to make it possible to do the novel," he said. She leaned across the kitchen table, so close he felt her breath on his face.

"Honey," his Muse said, "read my lips: that's what you *do*!"

"I mean it, go away," Batteiger said.

"Sure, love," she said, "if that's what you're sure you want right now. But can I sit on your lap a sec? Give us a little kiss bye?" Batteiger shut his eyes, thought about his novel, his writing table, legal pads, sharpened Ticonderogas, remembered lines from the semi-rave *Times* review of his first book.

She was gone when he allowed himself to look, but the echo of her chesty laughter hung in the air of his kitchen.

Batteiger sat at his writing table. He lit a Camel, sipped at his mug of coffee, picked up the Number 2 Ticonderoga, checked to see it was sharp enough. Then he set the pencil down, dragged on his cigarette, took another sip of coffee, picked up the pencil. Then he looked out the apartment window. The street, traffic. He laid the pencil down on the yellow pad, stood, walked through the apartment, just to be sure he was alone. He was alone, and there was no sound of laughter in the air, no odor of anything he did not know as his own; he sat again at his writing table, lit a fresh cigarette, made sure the coffee was still warm enough to drink, picked up the Ticonderoga, looked out the window, laid it down again.

So it went, day after day. If there was an important novel in him waiting to be freed, written, Batteiger could not locate it. If the experience of his failed marriage contained a story worth the telling, he could not remember it. If he had the imagination necessary to fabricate characters, narrative, a background for them, he was unable to tap into it. If there were words swimming in his brain like motes in sunlight, they eluded his grasp when he reached to order them in sentences, paragraphs.

He tried. He tried writing at his table with Ticonderogas and legal pads. He tried sitting up in his Murphy bed with a lapboard, out in the kitchen, seated on the commode, standing up, lying on the floor. He found copies of his two published novels, boxed and faded issues of the long-since defunct literary magazines that printed his early stories. He tried to read his canon, but the pages blurred, his attention wandered.

He thought to write his daughter again, but would not until he could afford another child support installment. He knew he would not call his agent until he had at least a chapter to show him, a rough synopsis. When the phone rang—he was sure it was Nate Schimpf wanting him to reconsider the ghosting job—Batteiger did not pick up the receiver.

Throat raw from chain-smoking Camels, stomach soured with coffee, he began to drink to keep from thinking about writing; that worked for a while, until he got maudlin, semi-hysterical. Then he drank himself insensible, did not know how long he lay, passed out, fully clothed, on the Murphy bed.

"Alma Jean," Batteiger said before he knew he was awake.

"Right here, baby," Batteiger's Muse said, "Mama's right here beside you, cuteness!" He sat up, seeming to remember a dream in which she kissed him awake; he rubbed at his lips as she laughed.

"Did you kiss me just now?" he asked. She sat next to him on the edge of the bed, leaned over him as he let himself lie back.

"Sometimes a gal just can't help herself for her hormones, you know?" she said. "I bet you're a super kisser when you're awake to put some oomph in it!" If she smelled bad, Batteiger thought, so must he, passed out who knew how long in clothes he hadn't changed for days.

"How tall are you?" he asked.

"A hair under six-two," his Muse said. "All woman and all yours, Batteiger," she said. "Think of it like those naked chubbies Rubens painted pictures of," she said when he closed his eyes.

"I'm an *artist*! I'm not a hack!" he said.

"La-de-dah," his Muse said; she swung her big legs up on the bed, lay beside him, head against his shoulder. "I like you fine the way you are."

"I've got two novels, the *Times* called me a contender."

"So the *Times* is some big Bible you believe everything you read?"

"I wrote what was in my heart!"

"So figure your heart's maybe abnormal small, you could've written it all out, you're just now finding out, Batteiger."

"I wrecked my marriage and lost my daughter because I was devoted to my craft." He began to cry.

"Everybody's selfish, just some more so is all," his Muse said.

He choked through his tears. "I wanted to leave my mark, be immortal through my language!"

"Immortal's not squat if you can't pay the rent, Batteiger."

"What's the point of living if you can't do what you want with your life?"

"What's the point," Batteiger's Muse said, "living if you don't do what you do best? You got to *write,* Batteiger, you're a *writer!* Here," she said, helping him up and off the bed, "Alma Jean's going to clean your face off for you, stop the waterworks now, Alma Jean's going to take care of her big writer guy, show you how nice I can be when I'm in the mood, huh?" And she led him to the bathroom, washed and dried his face, led him back to the Murphy bed.

Batteiger woke, suddenly fully alert, feeling better than he had for months, rested, healthy, optimistic. Beside him, Alma Jean snored like a freight train, stirred, snorted, resumed her snoring.

Today, he'd meet with Nate Schimpf and the stockbroker. After that, there was a contract for a series of biographies, the lives of pioneer oilmen, the money coming out of a Texas trust funded by a consortium set up to redeem the industry's public image. After that, Alma Jean teased, they might just take a fling on the West Coast, screenwriting.

Batteiger turned to his sleeping Muse, patted the great mound of her rump. She interrupted her snoring with a snort, like a pistol shot; it amazed him, how the heat of her body flowed into him!

He wondered how his daughter would take to Alma Jean when they met, if Grace would think of her as a new mommy, the way she thought of his ex's husband as a new daddy.

Whatever, Batteiger could confront the world with an honest face, honest money in his pocket. *A real writer,* he said to himself, *is one who gets paid for it!*

THE WAY YOU KNOW IN DREAMS

When I was in Vietnam, just before I rotated home, I had a dream one night about my Uncle Roy—he'd been dead at least a couple years before I enlisted. This happened, this dream I had, when I was on casual status assignment to Division's repo depot, which at the time was located near An Loc—Division brought me and some others out of the field early, back to the world, to wait on rotation date where a situation involved us in something. To avoid problems from this, I and these others were just waiting for rotation home, and I had this dream. It was very real to me.

Like all dreams, this one had lots in it didn't make sense or mean anything I can figure. In the dream we were up at my family's cottage on Long Lake, which in reality was sold years earlier, when my mother died. But it was the cottage and the lake where I spent whole summers for years when I was a kid and even part of high school. Lots of it was real, but mixed up with oddities, like any dream.

It was evening in the dream, and the cottage was filled with people, sort of a family reunion, which we had several of there over the years. But this was bigger, more people than ever there really were. There were people in my family still alive even now, my brothers, some cousins I haven't seen in ages, my two aunts, who were alive when I dreamed them, though dead now long since, and my Uncle Roy, of course already passed away.

It was an evening, very pleasantly cool after a hot summer day, a beautiful breeze coming in the open windows. When I tuned out the voices of people talking, I heard the summer evening sounds—the fine breeze in the pines and poplars outside, the lake lapping on the beach, the kind of chorus insects make in the grass at night up at Long Lake, the twang big bugs make hitting the window screens, attracted by the lights inside. In my dream the atmosphere of the cottage was very busy and happy, like a reunion party, but I don't remember any food or anything to drink the way it would really have been.

In dreams you know things without seeing them or being told. Part of the happiness of it was more people were coming, going to arrive any minute. There was more of the mix of things in this, because I know my mother and father, both deceased quite some time, were coming to join us soon, and a lot of my ancestors were coming with them, grandparents, great-aunts and uncles I never met, all dead a long time by the time I had this dream there near An Loc at Division's repo depot.

I got confused thinking about it over the years since, interpreting it. Some of the people alive in the dream were gone before I dreamed them, some alive are still alive, some alive then have passed on since, so that's complicated. It's been so many years, only a few are still alive, and it's logical, if I live long enough, I could end up the only one alive both in the dream and real life.

The main part I dreamed was of me and my Uncle Roy. So much of what else's in it is just the way you know in dreams, but the two of us I saw—*see*—and what we said also.

My Uncle Roy sat in a chair next to a small table, sort of in one corner of the cottage. There was a lamp on the table, and this light kind of covered just the two of us, everyone else, all the dead and still-alive relations away from us, happy in a kind of darkness that was the dark of dreams you can still see in if you want. I sat on the other side of this table from my uncle, sharing his special light, and we were in a way away from the reunion party going on, waiting for all the others to come.

I did all the actual talking in my dream, but it was as if I heard what Uncle Roy thought, as if he could speak to me without any words. I kept my eyes on him, watched closely all the time I talked to him. I talked to him about past family things—I was reminiscing because it was a reunion, and because also, just like he seemed to sit away from everyone else at his table, in the special lamp's light, it felt wrong to me, like he wasn't enjoying what he should at a reunion. I talked to him about past family things because I wanted the reunion to be the way it should be, sure he enjoyed it, so I could also.

I asked him if he could remember several things—the times he taught me to play card games he called *gambler's games,* casino and blackjack, stud poker; baseball games we listened to, Cubs and White Sox, all the old-time baseball greats he'd seen play in the flesh; when he taught me Morse code; his terrible ulcer operation in the days they cut three-fourths from your stomach out to cure them; the lessons in manners he gave me when I failed to hold my mother's chair when she went to sit down to dinner, to call him *sir* when I spoke to him. In this dream I said to him, *Uncle Roy, do you remember the time,* and *Do you remember how mad you got the time,* and *Tell me again about that time when.*

Each time I spoke, it was like he answered me, replied, said something like, *Of course I do,* or *That was a day I won't forget soon,* or *To a certitude,* something like that. But he was not speaking, even though I heard his voice as if he did. And every time I brought up something funny or ironic or strange from our family past, his expression showed he remembered—he half-smiled or nodded or shook his head, rolled his eyes.

The strangest part of it was what else I also knew the way you can in dreams. All this time I spoke, watching him very close, seeing him respond, hearing his answers in the special way, he was also looking away from me. Not at all the others gathered in the cottage, not out the windows where Long Lake lay, rippled by the breeze, the moon's reflection like broken mirror pieces on the water. What I knew was my Uncle Roy looked *back*, toward his own past times, back before I ever was, back to times and people only *he* could remember, so couldn't talk about to anyone.

And also I knew part of his half-smile or head shaking was over me, *at* me, because I didn't know, couldn't remember what he did, and everything I spoke about to him was okay, but it was only mine, not his, so we couldn't be there—*really*—together at that family reunion. It was just my dream of it.

I talked like that, what seemed a long time in dream-time, he nodded and smiled, really all by himself in the special light of the table's small lamp, and then I think I eventually realized the way we could not possibly be together there. It was a dream, and I think this woke me up, there near An Loc, sleeping on a cot under a tent-fly, in the sticky night-heat of Vietnam, waiting on casual assignment status for my rotation date to go home, away from there and those problems forever.

For all the fact I loved my family, as anyone would, I strangely enough turned out not to be what you'd call a family-type person. I mean, I loved my parents and brothers, aunts, uncles, cousins, normally enough all the time I was a kid growing up, as a young man also. From this dream alone it's clear we were a close family. We had several actual family reunions, up at the Long Lake cottage and other places too. Birthdays, Christmas, anniversaries, all were occasions in a big way. My one brother got married when I was in junior high, which was a very big family occasion, and when I got married, both times, family was there, all the ones still around.

The Way You Know in Dreams

Still, I can't say I'm the close family type. My first ex-wife I never see, nor my son from her, which I explain by how far away they live—she got married again, and I caused no hassle when that husband legally adopted the boy I have no contact with, who, for all I know, could possibly be married himself; he's old enough if he did it as young as I did. I feel funny thinking it's at least possible I'm a grandparent. I account for this first bad marriage on grounds I was too young, just out of the military and so on.

My second time I would have to take the major blame for divorcing. This ex-wife and my son from her live close, and I see them because I'm invited for family things like his birthday, and there's no new husband for her as yet—I go when invited, bring a present and behave decent, talk to them about how he's doing in school and sports, how's she doing on her job she has, answer her questions as to how I'm getting along with a straight face, but this second one is also not a *close* family to say the least. I pay child support but not alimony.

I admit over the years to getting the thought of contacting my first ex-wife and son, writing a letter, asking all the questions and saying some obvious things. But it's the same as when I visit the second ones by invitation for some occasion, I quickly realize there's nothing I care to say or hear. I end up shaking my head the way a trick horse counts, laughing at myself inside for being foolish.

I never see my brothers and their families, much less all the cousins I was so close with growing up in my family. Of course the previous generation is all gone long since.

At An Loc, waiting on rotation home, this general subject came up in various subtle and not-so-subtle ways. Firstly, the others from my unit pulled back out of the bush early would ordinarily have been people I'd be close to—we *were* close when we were out in the field, given circumstances of duty. At the An Loc repo depot, given our status, we didn't mix much. First they had us quartered away from administration and personnel shuttling in and out, so no close relations there, and then we related to each other only as necessary, so a kind of double non-closeness being there.

Secondly, in all the interviews, which were termed *exit orientation debriefing,* the general subject had a way of coming out. I talked with two people I strongly suspect were doctors, though they wore no medical brass on their fatigues. One, a major, was interested in the bush experience; the captain had some interest in my actual family background, and I assume this was the routine for all of us pulled out of the field early to wait rotation home there. We surely did not compare any notes among us.

For example, the major asked me, "Do you know anything of family structure in a hamlet like An Wan?"

"Which hamlet is that?" I asked, playing dumb as a standard procedure.

"*The* hamlet."

"I never knew its name. I think we called it a number as I recall. Also I can't recall the number we gave it."

"An Wan," the major said. "Whatever. My question is, do you know anything about the way families are organized there?"

"Meaning?" I said.

"That, for instance," this major said, "the way they live as a family group may be different from the way you, for instance, or me, how we define who's family and who's not."

"Aunts and uncles and the like?" I asked.

"Right. And grandparents and cousins, in-laws and so forth."

"Not the first thing," I told him. "And in fact I never considered them as being *families.*"

"Just dinks?"

"Not necessarily that word. I heard it, and *slope* and such, possibly used it myself in conversation."

The Way You Know in Dreams

"What," he asked me, "do you think might be potential possible implication of that nomenclature?"

"I know what *nomenclature* means," I said. "What I considered like anyone else probably is implications of hooches in the bush with only kids and women and old grannies on scene, which I knew to consider of significance when we came on scene, which anyone will tell you is procedure." This of course set him off on another track more interesting to him, which was the idea of playing dumb as a strategy.

Repo depot routine was fundamentally boring, but comfortable enough. We were set apart there with just tent-flys to sleep and eat and be in, so missed some of the things administrative and the transient casuals had for distraction, movies and a lending library and such, but our mess was good enough, the same rations everyone got, and we got and sent mail, and the beer ration, PX supplies available, so we had music from tape decks and so forth. Of course we didn't attend the orientations held for regular casual transient personnel, and though An Loc itself was absolutely secure, and administrative personnel went there to raise hell, we were expressly not allowed.

The boredom factor was significant. When I wasn't eating or interviewed, I sat or laid on my cot under the tent-fly, avoiding heat and sunlight and such rain as fell. I dozed a lot, and often pretended to be asleep, listening to tape deck music, watching others from my unit with my eyes slitted. They did the same. Everyone sat or laid around, sleeping or pretending, or looking off in the distance like there was something to be there—everybody thought their own thoughts of whatever, which is another way of accounting for how little except the necessary routine talk there was among us.

As I said, at this time I had this dream about my one uncle that seemed so very real. So laying around killing time at Division, I naturally thought some about him.

Uncle Roy was my oldest uncle, married my mother's oldest sister—they had no children because they got married so late in life. Oddly, as a kid I seemed to know more about my other uncles than about him. What little I knew about him I knew from some few clues in what he said to me, things he seemed to know something about.

For example, unlike the rest of my family, he came from somewhere in the South—Kentucky or Tennessee maybe. I gather he lost his father early, left home on his own when he was just a kid himself. He did a stint in the Navy, where he learned telegraphy, which is how he made his living for a long time, knocking around. I remember something he said once when we were playing cards—he taught me all the gamblers' games. We sat at his dining room table, playing casino or black-jack maybe. He kept score on a pad, in dollars, as if we played for real money. He was pretty mean about riding me, crowing about how much money I owed him, thousands. I asked him something, maybe how it was he knew so much about card games played for big money.

He squinted against the smoke from the cigarette in his mouth while he shuffled the deck, laid it in front of me for the cut—I was maybe nine or ten years old. He said, "Before I met your aunt and became civilized, I was what in that era was usually termed a *sport*."

"You did sports?" I said.

"Not exactly," he said.

"Then what?"

"A *sport*," my Uncle Roy said to me, "is a gent who indulges in amusements not deemed proper by civilized folk."

"Is that us?" I asked. "*Civilized?*"

"To the nth degree," he said, and he said, "rest assured you're not missing anything of value thereby. To the contrary."

I associated him with sports anyhow. He knew the card

games of gamblers, read a racing form, had seen championship prizefights, followed baseball, told me all about the Black Sox scandal, what was common knowledge and what was known only to insiders, people, he said, *in the know.* Things nobody else in my family seemed to know about.

"What were some of the amusements?" I said.

"Play your cards," my Uncle Roy told me, smirking at me through his cigarette smoke, shaking his head no, he wouldn't say.

The captain who interviewed me, near An Loc, who I am sure was also a doctor, was directly interested in my actual family at home.

"If you were to choose one of these," he said, "would you say your family life experience was happy, unhappy, in-between?"

"In what ways?" I said.

"All ways. Any respect comes to mind."

"Some of all. All three."

"Who's your favorite person in your family? If you were to pick a favorite member."

"I can't say. Why are you asking me this stuff?"

"Just cooperate," the captain said. He had a tape recorder going, same as the major-doctor. "So who?" he said.

"I couldn't say for sure. It would vary different times."

"Put another way," he said, "if you had to choose one member to die, who would that be?"

"Some already are," I said.

"Imagining for a second they're all still living and breathing."

"I can't," I said. "I can't wish anyone dead."

"I didn't say to *wish.* I'm talking hypothetical—pretending for the purposes of discussion."

"I understand *hypothetical,*" I told him, which sent him off asking me about my education, had I liked school, did I conceive of further education after I separated, what was my favorite subject in school, and the like. I played it dumb, which was our strategy. I don't think I or anyone told those doctors anything in all in the interviews we had there. To this day, if anyone cares, nobody knows the first thing about it.

But those interviews were the best possible training for all the talking I've been subject to since. The VA, for example, is very big on counseling, which means *talk*—talk about your active service, talk about since, jobs you had or want to get or just got, about your wives and your sons, about your family past, about everything in the world they can't possibly know anything about. *Talk.* Counseling, which is sometimes called *therapy,* is talking to various people who don't know anything you know, and wouldn't even if you tried to tell them instead of playing dumb.

In the end you get what you want, or at least need, anyhow. However, I think they *think* they know a lot about me, VA counselors and therapists and so-called community resource persons.

One thing I am *not* is one of the professional whiners. Anything I've had to do with any of it since I rotated home was because I was compelled, required to check in wherever and talk with them, listen to all the talk, be interviewed about my life then and since. Which is price enough to pay, in my estimation. I come into contact with hundreds of others at the VA, for example, and all I felt is embarrassed for and by them. There are about three main types, and I have no use for any.

There are all the slick ones, ones making their living off it, off me and the others they call in to talk, VA and political types. They are very clean and neat—slick. They sit back, wearing white smocks because they're doctors now, and they say things like, *I know what I'm talking about when we discuss this, you know,* they say, *I pulled my tour the same as you did, I have no difficulty in empathizing,* they say.

The Way You Know in Dreams

I play dumb with them, say, *Really. Where were you in country?* They say, *We operated out of Long Binh,* or, *I was in the Mekong when it hit the fan,* or *Up near the DMZ some,* and such.

Playing dumb, I say, *I was never in that arena of operations,* or *That was after my time,* or just *Do tell.* The really slick types are elected in Congress or governors or run the Washington bureau offices of the VA—you can see them on television, so neat and clean, getting elected. They can't tell me a thing any more than I can them.

I'm most seriously embarrassed by the types who parade. How embarrassing to see them dress up in old fatigues all tricked out with ribbons and patches, carrying flags and unit guide-ons, chanting and raising their fists, giving speeches at monuments into microphones in the wind, *an ungrateful and uncaring nation* and so on. Some of them with eye patches, empty sleeves, on crutches, in wheelchairs—but they're old and fat now, wear their hair too long, facial hair, a kind of public whining I find disgusting. The last place I could be found is standing at that wall, feeling the names cut in the stone like a blind man reading with his fingers, laying flowers and blubbering while somebody blows a bugle—*never!*

I, no doubt, appear little different from the others sitting around the lounges waiting for our names to be called. We are all fat and old, smoke a lot of cigarettes, rarely speak to each other. They sit around smoking or with their heads in their hands, and if anybody talks to anybody else, it is whining. *I'm making it, I think,* or *I can't seem to get it together,* or *My lady is hassling me,* etcetera. It's talk to kill time waiting for your name to be called out, so you sit quiet and think about whatever it is only you have to think about. I probably appear like one of these, but have nothing to say to any of them, think my own thoughts. Lots are just dopers crashing.

I dwell on my Uncle Roy. Nobody in the family who might

actually have known the true facts of his life are around any more to tell it, but there were some sort of *rumors,* I'd call them. Beyond being a *sport*—which I assume means he gambled and raised general holy hell, that is. My memory is he was supposed to have been involved in worse once upon a time.

For example, he seemed to talk like he knew a lot about the gangsters of Chicago way back. Once, I forget how it came up, he had me stand up—I was a kid, ten or so—so he could show me how a gangster named O'Bannion was shot to death by some other gangster in his flower shop in Cicero, Illinois. He had me shake hands with him, then held my hand tight while he pretended to draw a gun and shoot me with his free hand. "That's your gun hand I'm holding," he said. He said, "O'Bannion didn't have a chance, the stupid Harp!"

"Neat," I said.

"It accomplished the task admirably," my uncle said. He also once told me he boarded at a rooming house with a man he knew well enough to take rides in his car; it was an old car, but the engine souped up. "Take a flyer on a guess as to where that jamoke ended up," he said to me.

"I give up," I said.

"On the floor," my Uncle Roy said, "of a certain automotive garage on a certain morning that just happened to be St. Valentine's Day."

"I don't get it."

My uncle said, "He sure did. It's too complicated to explain," he said, and grinned at me, shuffled the deck for another hand.

I asked my mother about that. I said, "Was Uncle Roy some kind of gangster?"

"What?" she said, looked at me. I waited for her to say something, but she didn't. She looked away, like there was something else she had to see. Then she said, "Lord save us from little pitchers," and shook her head, told me to go do a chore or something to get me off the subject. I doubt she knew any more about it than I did.

In my family, probably coming from Depression days hard times before even my parents, there was a strong work ethic. They were very prejudiced against people taking welfare—I understand and appreciate it, because that came from their experience. I'm not.

I get my disability at a post office box, and when I go down to get it, I'm tempted strongly to take the envelope and put it on the floor right there in the post office, get down on the floor and roll on it, like a dog does with something decayed. I figure it's mine, I have it coming—without any whine about it! Feel not the slightest trace of shame.

The closest to an actual clue I have about my Uncle Roy comes from a story he half-told me once when we were playing casino. He caught me cheating on my count when I laid down —I had had it with him beating me so bad, crowing about all the supposed money I owed him.

"Cheat a man at cards," he said to me, "you either better learn more finesse or be prepared to suffer consequences."

"I'm sorry," was all I could think to say.

"Sorry does not feed the bulldog."

"I won't do it again."

"Do and I'll rap you one'll make your head ring."

"I promise," I said. I was almost crying—I was maybe eleven.

"Shoeless Joe and his cohorts got off lucky," my uncle said, "I could tell you a story of a man wasn't so fortunate."

"Tell me," I said, because I could barely stop from crying, wanted to get him off the subject of my cheating, afraid he'd tell my aunt or my parents or brothers.

"Back in the Stone Age," Uncle Roy said, pausing to light a

cigarette, fill the air between us with smoke, look up at his dining room ceiling like there was a movie running there he could see, describe to me.

"Back in the Stone Age," he repeated, "I mustered out of the Navy and shipped out of Frisco as radio man on a vessel plying the maritime trade in the Pacific." He paused again, smiled to himself. "Now Frisco," he said, "was a town then offering amusements for a sporting gent, I could tell you if you were a tad older. Be that as it may," he said, shook his head, "I shipped out and soon took up the regular practice of cutthroat poker with several of my cohorts of like inclination."

"What's *inclination*?" I asked.

"Am I telling this or are you?"

"You are."

"Never interrupt," Uncle Roy said, "when a man's telling you a parable of moral instruction." I didn't ask him what *parable* meant.

My Uncle Roy said, "A particular jamoke who joined us in this pastime soon emerged the big winner, and I and others quickly found ourselves writing markers on wages we wouldn't collect until voyage's termination back in Frisco. Needless to say, this caused me no end of consternation." He paused, frowned, as if he dared me to interrupt again. "Consternation led to curiosity, which in turn led me to observe this character, who worked as a slavey in the ship's galley, possessed less dexterity than he supposed. Are you following me?" he asked me.

"He wasn't finessed enough," I said.

"Indeed. At which juncture I shared this information with a couple other jamokes equally indebted to this cheating cook's helper. We agreed on a plan of action which entailed accosting this person late of an evening on a portion of the cargo deck not visible from the watch on the bridge, sailing near the coast of an island called Borneo."

"I know where that's on a map," I said, horrified I interrupted him again, but he went on, as if he was talking to himself, looking at the ceiling.

"The affair was complicated due to this jamoke packing a Colt repeater. However, I, for my part, was partial to what was called an *imported Italian hunting knife*—switchblade to you—kept in my boot. Suffice it to say my dexterity was superior to his when push came to shove. Literally." My uncle closed his eyes, was silent until I spoke.

"What happened?" I said—I was possibly eleven years old.

Uncle Roy's eyes popped open, he looked at the ceiling, looked at me, almost a surprised expression on his face, like he didn't expect to find me there, listening.

"You're too young to hear it," he said.

"Please!"

"Suffice to say the game is called *cutthroat* for a reason, and bear in mind the waters of Borneo were and probably still are known for sharks, who don't play poker, so aren't fussy what they eat."

"You stabbed him and sharks ate him?"

"Your deal," Uncle Roy said, nudged the deck across the table to me. "Keep in mind I'm scrutinizing you," he said.

Now this is no more than a clue, because he didn't tell me anything for a fact. Also I consider the possibility he made it up entirely, to impress me not to cheat at cards, or just amuse a kid. But it's also possible he meant to try and tell me something he perhaps never told anyone, never could. I'll never know.

What I end up with is no more certain or factual than the dream of my uncle I had, there near An Loc, Division repo depot, soon after which I rotated home, away from those problems, into new ones, the rest of my life to now, etcetera.

Oddly, though I think so often of my Uncle Roy, and of my one dream of him that happened long after he was dead and gone, I never dreamed of him ever again. Like anyone, I dream all the time when I sleep, and my dreams, some of them, are crazy as anyone's. Some are about real things and people from my entire life—my childhood, my family, when I was in country in Vietnam, even those hooches I was told were called An Wan—my life since, my two ex-wives and two sons, one from each—some are like real life, some pure crazy, some mixed, too complicated to explain.

I've been requested, countless times, to tell my dreams—I say I can't remember, play dumb. The fact is, I pay a lot of attention to dreams—I have the belief they'll teach me something. I have the belief I'll learn something in a dream I can't find out otherwise, anywhere, from anyone.

MODERN HISTORY

The most memorable episode in my life involves a man—a high school boy—named John Henry Ruttman. I say *memorable,* not *significant,* because the episode was so horribly inexplicable beneath its surface that significance—import, *meaning*—is absolutely unimaginable. At best, I label it an instance of sheer insanity. If there is, in the case of John Henry Ruttman, some point or purpose I have yet to apprehend, I fear it must be so dark I am better served not to glimpse or grasp it, that I will do well to leave it forever among all that mass of personal trivia I cannot relate to the short arc of history's sweep within which I exist.

I have lived well over half my possible life; I have no idea if John Henry Ruttman still lives, or if he died, when, where, how. And if John Henry Ruttman is still alive, I cannot conceive where he might be—still imprisoned or released, paroled, cured. As I think about this, it is not at all improbable, if he still lives, that John Henry Ruttman leads a quite normal life, married, a parent like me. Perhaps even a grandparent also by this time?

I was born in the latter days of the Great Depression, so have no experience of it, though my parents, even my much-older brother, spoke often of it. So I have their anecdotes:

My father owned a rattle-trap Ford, which, when he was out of work, he used to transport neighbors to and from locations in Milwaukee where commodities (peanut butter, rice, lard) were distributed to the eligible destitute, charging each passenger a quarter; my mother told me of the time she gave my brother a dime, sent him to the butcher's to buy three hamburger patties—he was waylaid by two older boys who took the money, there was no supper in our home that night; my brother never forgot the teasing he suffered at school for his tennis shoes, rotting canvas patched with black masking tape.

They are anecdotes, no more than that, mean nothing to me.

I grew up during the Second World War, and from this time, personal, *real* moments remain. I know I heard my parents discuss the war, and I read newspaper headlines, watched the newsreels at Saturday matinees, and remember a fifth grade teacher going to the blackboard to explain to us how it was the Germans had broken our lines in the Ardennes. But there is no *life* for me in these fragments, no *meaning*.

What lives for me—though I cannot imagine what the meaning might be—are the immediacies:

My brother was drafted in 1942, and I was embarrassed to be told by my mother to give him a goodbye kiss as we stood beside the olive drab bus that took him to Fort Sheridan, Illinois; we hung a blue-star service flag in our front window; my father found a very good job as a machinist, making precision artillery shell casings; my mother rolled cigarettes for my father with a little metal box of a machine because Lucky Strike Green had gone to war; I flattened empty tin cans for my mother, contributed to scrap drives; she saved cooking fat to turn in to the butcher in exchange for meat-ration coupons; my father bought a better car, a used LaSalle, but could not drive it much because tires and gasoline were also rationed; we sat together, my parents and I, while my mother read my brothers V-mail letters to us with a magnifying glass; I saw a huge poster in the store window, caricatures of Hitler, Tojo, Mussolini dancing, hands linked, in a circle—a large X drawn over the figure of Il Duce, the caption: *One Down, Two to Go!;* I once lost a roll of dimes my mother gave me to take to school to buy red Defense Savings Bond stamps; when my brother was killed in the Battle of the Bulge, we took down the blue-star flag, replaced it with gold.

If there were some pattern, a design, to it, there would of course be meaning in it, but John Henry Ruttman came into my life by chance. It was 1951: I was a first-semester freshman at Riverside High School.

There were twenty-seven of us in Miss Myrna Leet's homeroom, the class where we reported each morning to be counted present, receive printed handouts, hear the vice-principal's announcements and admonitions over the intercom. Assigned in pairs to share hall lockers that held our coats and jackets, it was only chance I ended up the odd number, no locker partner from my homeroom. And pure chance John Henry Ruttman, a senior, the odd number in his homeroom just down the hall—blind chance we were assigned to share one of the metal cabinets with a combination lock mid-way between our two homerooms. The school's system segregated students by class—freshman, sophomore, junior, senior—but chance brought us together, introduced by Miss Myrna Leet at our locker. She gave us each a slip of paper with the lock's combination on it—brought John Henry Ruttman and me together in contradiction of our school's simple plan for the orderly disposition of its students by age, class standing, homeroom assignment.

Miss Myrna Leet told him my name, said, "This is John Ruttman. John's a senior. He'll graduate next spring, so he'll tell you all the rules for using your locker between your classes and during lunch period," and I remember we stood in silence; I suppose she expected us to shake hands, like two adults? John

Henry Ruttman, a wholly blank, bored expression on his face, seemed to look through me, and I did not know how I was supposed to look at him, what to do. Then he nodded to me—at me—as if he had been told to look until he found something. I knew to nod back, and that was how we met.

"I'll leave you two to talk a minute," said Miss Myrna Leet, and left us, but we said nothing. John Henry Ruttman opened the combination lock, tossed his books on the single chest-high shelf, hung his jacket on one of the two hooks set in either side below the shelf; then he nodded, pointed at the floor of the locker—that was where I was to put my books. Then he left to go back to his homeroom.

"Are we all arranged to share our locker with a member of the graduating class?" Miss Myrna Leet asked when I returned to her room.

"Sure," is all I said to her.

"Memorize your combination first thing," she said to me.

That is how I came to know John Henry Ruttman, who is the most important memory of my life, at least as I try to think about its larger meaning. What is telling is that it could as well have been two other students assigned to share a locker, freshman and senior, something not contained in our school's system governing the use of hall lockers.

I try to remember what was happening in the world outside high school, beyond my neighborhood, the city of Milwaukee. I read both the morning *Sentinel* and the afternoon *Journal*, listened to the radio with my parents, and every freshman student was required to take a kind of civics class in which current events were discussed. I remember only generalities.

The Cold War was in full force; newscasters and headlines called Stalin *Uncle Joe*; Uncle Joe had the atomic bomb, and we tested new ones near Las Vegas; the Rosenbergs had been tried, convicted, executed; a new real war, called a *conflict,* began in Korea—first we were losing it, then winning, and MacArthur was a hero again, for Inchon; then the Chinese entered the war, and we were losing it again; Truman fired MacArthur, and everyone despised Harry Truman—L.S.M.F.T. now meant *Lord Save Me From Truman;* my parents wore Taft buttons for the 1952 election campaign; Eisenhower won because he promised to go to Korea if elected, and he did; our junior senator, Joe McCarthy, was famous or infamous—my father liked him; my mother didn't.

What I remember clearly are my parents, their growing estrangement from one another. We listened to the radio together in the evenings, but when they talked about the news, they betrayed the rift between them that widened all through my high school years.

"Wonderful," my father said about the Korean Conflict. "Wilson promises his boys won't fight on foreign soil, I wind up in France. Franklin Rosenfeldt kills my first boy, this goddamn little Pendergast Machine haberdasher's setting up to take my last one. It's a damn plot."

"Don't say stupid things," my mother said.

"Stupid yourself if you don't see it," he said to her. When these moments occurred, I was stricken with panic that transformed into a searing rage if I could not interrupt them, divert them, think of something to say to break their momentum.

"There's this guy's a junior," I said, "I heard he's quitting school, his parents signed so he can enlist in the Marines."

"So much for the peanut gallery heard from," my father said; I hated him in a moment like this, wished for the strength to hurt him.

"You can be such a fool," my mother said, and I hated her for provoking him further. "If Truman doesn't stop it, the Republicans will."

"Ike," my father said, baring his teeth. "Listen to the woman! *Ike*," he said, "is in the business of making wars last I heard, but then what the hell do I know, right?" he said as if inviting her to take her turn.

"I have to do homework!" I shouted to stop them, to smother the fire of rage roaring within me.

I do not know enough about John Henry Ruttman to say he was either unusual or very ordinary as high school seniors went, then. I know he had good friends in the senior class, saw him with them—walking to and from classes in the halls, waiting for him at our shared locker when we came at the same time to pick up and drop off books between classes, and, of course, the last night I saw him, at the basketball game. But I never spoke to his friends, he did not introduce us, so I know almost nothing about the sort of high school senior he was. My suspicion is he was very ordinary—a seventeen-year-old senior at Milwaukee's Riverside High School in 1951.

What made a particular impression on me whenever I saw him was his appearance, and the inevitable blank, impenetrable expression on his face.

John Henry Ruttman was tall, over six feet, and because I was small for my age, seemed enormous to me, the way my father—though he was not a tall man—seemed enormous, even when I stood close to him, saw he was not much taller than I. John Henry Ruttman seemed like an adult to me.

He had a small, very light brown moustache, the only student I saw in high school who wore a moustache—I am certain this was not allowed back then, but somehow he had a moustache. He had long, thick sideburns—fashion then—and long hair, but did not wear it in the ducktail cut everyone else effected; John Henry Ruttman parted his hair in the middle, the way men my father's age, or older, wore their hair. He looked much older than seventeen.

When he looked at me, looked at the combination lock, twirled its dial, looked at his textbooks to find the one for his next class, looked at his friends who waited at the locker for him, his face revealed not the slightest interest in anything or anyone. It was as if he was, really, as old as he appeared to me, as if no person or thing or moment had any conceivable relevance for his life, as if he was already preoccupied with profound, adult matters, lost in contemplation, distracted by thoughts I could never dream of conceiving. In his presence—a few minutes together at our shared locker, passing in the halls, at that basketball game the last time—I felt the way I did in my father's presence.

He intimidated me, frightened me, made me so angry the way my father did, or my mother—because I suspected, was sure, there were things going on that would surely affect me, withheld, but threatening. I always felt as though I ought to say something to him when we met at the locker, make him recognize me, respond, confide whatever secret, affirm something, but I was unable; I spoke only if he did first. Our greetings and goodbyes both were usually accomplished with nods—his, then mine—so I never knew what, if anything, he thought about that gave him his expression of maddening, transcendent indifference.

When I try to think about all the years since, I cannot make it coherent; I suppose I should read, study this history, learn to render it a straightforward narrative to make sense of the span of my life. But this is not the understanding I want. What I want, seek, is its center, some key explaining it all, explaining me to myself, and this I cannot seem to find.

There are the wars: the Second World War of my childhood

that killed my brother; the war in Korea they called a conflict and a police action when I was in high school; Vietnam, so protracted it feels like a generation of war; all the other wars—Biafra, the Falklands, Iran-Iraq, Afghanistan, Cambodia, Northern Ireland, where the war has endured centuries, El Salvador and Nicaragua, so many, big and small, short, long.

There were urban riots, black people burning Washington, Detroit, Los Angeles, shot for looting; assassinations, the Kennedys, Martin Luther King, attempts against Wallace, Reagan, thousands of Latin Americans and Arabs and Africans and Asians slaughtered and starved.

And prosperity and poverty, simultaneous and in cycles, oil dearths and gluts, money so inflationary it might be the currency of a child's board game, stock booms and busts, insider trading and green-mail, fraud so blatant it defies a name, and the endemic corruption of all politics—Watergate, Chappaquiddick, a host of congressmen and senators so venal they seem to me a faceless, nameless quotidian horde.

I confuse all these events when I try to order them, as if the Great Depression into which I was born and the world war of my childhood have never ended, only transformed into one grandly vicious, unbroken pageant of humanity's frail cruelty, fed on a plague of drugs, sung in raucous music, a babble of sincere obfuscation thrown back in our faces by the banal marvel of media until we no longer see ourselves in any of it—I see myself, all of us, sickening in the throes of new, incurable diseases, indifferently stupid. . . .

I cannot make *sense* of all the years since then!

I can think about my own life, about my parents—they divorced after nearly forty years of marriage; my father remarried a crazy woman, died painfully of colon cancer; my mother declined quickly, died slowly in a nursing home of what we now call Alzheimer's.

I can try to think only about my own life, but find nothing in it either, and become so frustrated, so angry I want to scream, strike at something!

What I catch myself returning to in my thoughts is John Henry Ruttman.

When I think about John Henry Ruttman, I think also of the rigidly uncodified, unspoken social rules ordering our lives at Riverside High School in Milwaukee, Wisconsin, in 1951. Everything—*everything!*—was prescribed or proscribed, and this made all our lives easier to live, made us secure in this matrix, told us clearly who we were, how we were to be, what we must and dare not do.

I knew how I must dress and behave and even speak if I were to live as a high school freshman. My hair was cut short on top, long on the sides, combed in the obligatory ducktail in back; my trousers were pegged, my bright-colored long-sleeve shirts buttoned to my neck, collar up in back, my suede or black spade-toe shoes uncleaned; I wore a bomber jacker. My friends were classmates—I did not presume to address an upperclassman unless first spoken to. I used the jargon: *fag* for cigarette, *hardly* to mean absolutely, *I'm sick* to mean I was delighted or thrilled, *bread* for money . . . I have forgotten most of the language I was required to speak.

In this way, I was secure in the life of my high school, and in this way I would, in time, become a senior like John Henry Ruttman, become an adult, enter into the wider world of experience and meaning awaiting us all, where I would be secure and comfortable forever.

So it was, because pure, inscrutable chance made us locker partners, I looked to John Henry Ruttman to learn what and who to be. I spoke when he spoke to me, meeting at our locker, listened to remember anything he might say, like the story of the junior who quit school to join the Marines and fight in Korea. I dressed as John Henry Ruttman did, despaired because I lacked the courage to part my hair down the center of my head, because I had neither the hope nor the courage to grow thick sideburns, much less a moustache.

And when he did not speak, only nodded to me, I returned his nod. When I walked the halls between classes, encountered him with a group of his good friends, fellow-seniors, I knew better than to speak or wave wearily; I waited on him, and John Henry Ruttman always nodded, turned his head a spare degree in my direction, unhooded his disdainful eyes for just an instant, and nodded to me—as if to say: *hello; you're doing it right; keep it up, you'll be what I am; we know who and what we are, everything as it should be, will be.*

The older I grow, well over half my life behind me, there is less and less I understand of what has become of me. Everything seems a kind of accident. Why did I go to college, study what I did? Why did I marry my first wife? How did I come to earn so much money so early in life, have such wonderful children—son and daughter—and why did it all go so bad so quickly? To what end did I abandon my wife and wonderful children, marry another? Is there some reason my son drowned on his eleventh birthday, my daughter married a very bad man she will not abandon? What made me think it right to marry again, a bad woman who abandoned me? Is there a lesson in my inability to earn much money now? Is there a text somewhere, a sermon can tell me why, to what end the whole of my life as I think on it now?

On a Friday night, late in the winter of 1951, I went with some of my friends to a high school basketball game; I do not recall who Riverside played, but it was the other team's gym.

We arrived early, took seats high in the bleachers, watched the warm-up—I cannot imagine what we might have talked about.

The warm-up over, the teams assembled at their benches, stripped off their jackets, huddled with their coaches, referees waiting with the ball at center court; I remember a kind of humming, the crowd gathering itself to cheer when line-ups were introduced. In that moment of muted talk and laughter, pep bands waiting to play fanfares, John Henry Ruttman, with several of his senior class friends, entered the gym.

They walked slowly, with the sure arrogance of seniors, along the edge of the court, slouched, hands in pockets, bomber jackets thrown open, scanning the bleachers as they moved closer to me; they looked, I suppose, for a block of open seats in the crowd, or for other friends already there. As they approached me, John Henry Ruttman's searching eyes met mine, recognized me.

Of course he did not wave or smile a greeting. He nodded, face adultly expressionless, inscrutable, the nod he gave me when we met at our shared locker, as we passed in the halls between classes; of course I returned his nod, my expression the mirror of his, as I had learned to do, and I knew, a last time, that stay of peace and security against whatever confused or frightened or frustrated me, felt, a last time, the tangible certainty that I knew who and what I was, would be for the rest of my life.

What I know of what John Henry Ruttman did that night, before coming to the basketball game with his friends, I know from reading the *Journal* and *Sentinel* coverage, from the told and retold rumors racing for weeks afterward through Riverside High School. Perhaps, now, I only imagine some of it?

John Henry Ruttman's father traveled in his work, sold or represented something in the cities and towns of southern Wisconsin, northern Illinois and Iowa and Indiana. He left Milwaukee that evening on business, promising his son the use of the family's second car to go to the game, drive his friends there, to go out after the game. After John Henry Ruttman's father left, he and his mother argued about something, and she denied him the use of the car, took the keys from him, forbade him to go to the game.

She stood at their kitchen sink, washing, rinsing, stacking supper dishes to dry in a rack. John Henry Ruttman went to his parents' bedroom, found his father's shotgun, loaded it, went to the kitchen, shot his mother in the back of the head as she stood at the sink. His younger brother and sister may have seen this, certainly heard the blast; John Henry Ruttman shot his mother a second time as she lay on the kitchen linoleum. His little brother and sister tried to hide from him, but their screaming led him to them, first his sister, then his brother.

His sister ran to their parents' bedroom, crouched down behind the clothes hanging in their closet. John Henry Ruttman slid the hanging clothes aside. She covered her eyes with her hands, screaming, before he shot her, also twice, where she crouched on the closet floor.

He had to look in several rooms before he found his little brother, who crawled under a parlor daybed. The daybed's slipcover hung down close to the floor. John Henry Ruttman knelt, lifted it, saw where his brother curled against the wall, barely enough space between the floor and bed to hold him; John Henry Ruttman probed under the bed with the gun's barrel, poked the muzzle tightly up against his brother's squirming body, shot him to death.

Then John Henry Ruttman showered and changed his clothes, because he was splattered with the blood of his mother and sister and brother; then he took blankets from his own bed, hammer and nails from a tool drawer, tacked blankets over some—not all—of the house's windows. Then he found where his mother put the car keys, left without locking the doors, drove away, picked up his friends, drove to the basketball game.

All this he had done, within the hour, when our eyes met and we exchanged our obligatory nods at the basketball game. We exchanged the greeting, our means of recognizing one another's presence, existence, relationship; then he looked away, slouched on, hands in pockets, with his friends, found seats in the bleachers far enough away that I could not see him, and I turned back to my friends where we sat, talked, watched the game. Of course I never saw him again, except for pictures of him in the newspapers.

After the game, John Henry Ruttman bought a case of beer, because he could pass for much older with his moustache, drove his friends, five in all, to Whitnall Park, where they drank the beer. Then he drove each friend to his house. In the newspapers, they all said they could not believe it; he said nothing, acted in no way differently. Then he drove out of the city, fled.

His father returned late the next day, and John Henry Ruttman was arrested, driving through St. Louis—the newspapers said he did not know where he was driving to, said the only reason he gave for what he did was that his mother made him mad when she denied him the car, and he had to kill his brother and sister because they knew he killed his mother. The newspapers said he did not say much, ever, expressed no remorse, no emotion of any sort.

John Henry Ruttman was judged mentally deranged, confined indefinitely, a trial postponed until such time as he might be judged competent to cooperate in his defense. If this ever happened, I do not know of it. I finished high school, went to college, married, followed the course of my life.

Because I cannot find answers, meaning, in either my life or the context of history with which I coexist, I make an effort not to dwell on any of this. It is not very often I think of this. When I do, I try very hard to make myself stop, just get on with living what life is left to me. I do not like to think of this—my life, history—because there is nothing to be gained, no peace of mind to be had unless and until I can—as eventually I always manage to do—forget it, put it out of my thoughts, get on with what is left of my life.

LIE-A-FORNIA

The man replied, "Things as they are
Are changed upon the blue guitar."

—Wallace Stevens

Looking back—over forty years now—I would be hard pressed to distinguish what, of all I remember, was truth, what falsehood, how much of it might be some amalgam of the two, one bleeding over into the other, changing, informing, reshaping—a truth tainted by only a small lie, a great fabrication given probability, even dignity, by some scrap of veracity.

Two facts: his name was Clarence Hall Cross (he always gave his full name, and his mother called him home to supper each evening from their front porch, slippered feet set wide, hands cupping her mouth for the megaphone effect); he lived, before his family moved into our neighborhood on Locust Street, in California, an exotic and immeasurably distant place in the Wisconsin of that era (both his mother and his father said this, and Miss Erna Haas, our fifth grade teacher at Hartford Elementary, announced it to us all when she introduced him to our class his first day with us).

Beyond that, after all this time, I cannot, will not swear to anything. Except to say he was the biggest, most outrageous liar I have ever known. And because *Clarence* was universally considered a name too stupid to utter, and because we knew he came from California, and because he was a liar of bizarre, absurd proportions, we all—I, my brothers Art and Freddie, everyone at school and in the neighborhood who knew him—called him Lie-A-Fornia. He did not particularly object.

"Lie-A-Fornia," we said once we knew him, "tell us again where it was you were born?"

"I was born," he said, "on the Isle of Capri."

"That's funny, last time we asked you you said Tampico, Mexico."

"I never," he said. "The Isle of Capri. My dad and mom went on a vacation there to go fishing there. You can catch bluegills weigh six, seven pounds in the lakes on the Isle of Capri, which is how's come I happened to be born there."

"Sure thing, Lie-A-Fornia," we said, "so you probably just forgot when you said Mexico last time, right, Lie-A-Fornia?"

"I lived in Tampico, Mexico, when I was little," he said. "My dad and mom moved us there right after I was born because he got a job at a gold mine—I was born on the Isle of Capri. I would of been born in Tampico, Mexico, except for my dad and mom going fishing for bluegills there on their vacation, but I lived in Tampico, Mexico, before we moved here."

"What happened to California where you moved from before here, Lie-A-Fornia!" we sneered.

"I did come here from California. I told you once, we moved to California from Tampico, Mexico, and some other places also because my dad got different jobs. And the name's Clarence Hale Cross, okay?"

"Okay," we said—I was ten, my brothers Art and Freddie twelve and thirteen and a half—"Okay, Lie-A-Fornia, whatever you say!" We badgered him, laughed at him, but he never got angry, never changed his story until the next time, never *ever* admitted to any of his preposterous lies.

"Clarence Hale Cross!" his mother shouted from their front porch. "Clarence Hale Cross! Supper! Time for supper!" she called out to all of Locust Street.

"Your ma's calling you, Lie-A-Fornia," we said. "Go on home before we de-pants you, you big fat liar-face!"

"My mom," he said over his shoulder to us as he ran for his porch, "used to sing operas in New York before she was my mom, which is why she's got such a strong voice!"

His father's unlimited number of unusual occupations (gold miner, prize-fighter, combat pilot, detective, mountain-climbing guide, scientist . . .), his mother's earlier careers (opera diva, movie actress, circus tightrope walker, model, Olympic pentathlon athlete, wine-taster, French chef . . .), his place of birth, his many foreign residences, rare pets he owned; there was nothing he would not lie about—history both ancient and modern, politics, the economy, feats of engineering, freaks of nature, popular entertainers, the weather of the day and of the approaching season. No subject was too grandiose or trivial to escape the embellishment of his invariably forked tongue. What made him memorable, then and now, was the enormity of the gulf between what he said and the hopelessly bland, quotidian surface of such evidence of the truths of his life as we could discover.

His father was, I think, a roundhouse switchman, maybe even only a gandy, in the Milwaukee Road yards. I knew he rode the streetcar to and from his work, saw him waiting for his line at the closest stop on the corner of Locust and Maryland, dressed in a denim coat and overalls, thick, oil-stained shoes, black lunch bucket in hand. Mr. Cross was, even to my ten-year-old eye, a dull, gross man. My father drove a pre-war Plymouth, worked in the clerk of civil court's office downtown, wore a necktie, suit, and fedora.

Mr. Cross used snuff, inserted a pinch in each black nostril with the tip of his dirty thumb. When he was at home (on standby, Lie-A-Fornia called it), Mr. Cross worked in his backyard. Theirs was the only house in the neighborhood with a vegetable garden. When he worked, turning over his sod with a pitchfork, he wore suspenders to hold up his torn trousers, what we then called a union suit (his underwear in every temperature). He stopped his planting or spading frequently to take his tin of Copenhagen from his pocket, sneezed, blew his nose with his fingers, then flicked them clean against his leg.

"So what you got growing?" I asked Lie-A-Fornia as we stood at the edge of his father's neat plot.

"Rare herbs," Lie-A-Fornia said.

"Look like damn radishes to me," my brother Art said.

"What's herbs?" I asked.

"Radishes and carrots," Art said.

"I only know Latin names you wouldn't recognize," Lie-A-Fornia said. "You use them to make medicine. My dad was going to be a doctor for a while before I was born, except he quit to go join up in the war in Spain."

"Bull," Art said.

"Where was that again? I asked. "You were born at?"

"Java," Lie-A-Fornia said. "We had a plantation we grew coffee on. We used elephants to pull the plow."

"Mr. Cross," I once asked his father, "I was wondering, your kid says you were in the Spanish Civil War."

"So what if he did?" is all he said. Then he said, "Don't putz around in my yard by yourself here, huh? I got tools in my shed I don't want you futzing with, huh, kid?"

Mr. Cross also drank. Playing in the last light of early evening, we watched him stagger up Locust Street from the direction of Bette & Dad's Tavern on Newberry, oblivious to us, muttering loudly to himself, swinging his arms viciously at whatever ghosts tormented him as he made his way home—this happened at least once a week. His son turned his back on the sight, pretended not to see or hear—something, of course, we could not allow.

"Lie-A-Fornia," we said, "catch your old man, he's about to fall on his big duff."

"That's road-work he's doing," Clarence Hale Cross said. "I told you he was the sparring partner once for Billy Conn, the light-heavyweight almost beat Louis. It's how you train to box."

"You said Barney Ross before," we reminded him.

"Him too," Lie-A-Fornia said. "Billy Conn fired him because he knocked Conn down sparring with him, so he did it for a while for Barney Ross and then quit to study flying lessons."

"Lie-A-Fornia," we said, "who the hell's he talking to?" Mr. Cross, weaving and bobbing, shuddering like a fighter trying to clear his head and get his legs back, screamed his incomprehensible threats and taunts up at the darkening sky.

"He's practicing," Lie-A-Fornia said, "his foreign language. My dad speaks twelve languages perfect and some more almost as good."

"So what language's he practicing, Lie-A-Fornia?" we asked as his father half-fell up his porch steps, then lurched to his front door.

"Nipponese," Lie-A-Fornia said as his mother opened their door and his father tumbled inside. "Which is about the hardest one to learn. During the war he worked on codes for the Navy, he speaks it so perfect."

"You said he worked on the atom bomb for the war," we told him.

"That too. After the Jap codes he broke," he said. "I gotta go now, my mom's probably too busy to call for me, she's working on a portrait of me she's painting." And he ran from us, as though deaf to our jeering.

Less frequently, later in the night as my brothers and I listened to radio serials or played spit-in-the-ocean, we heard the noise from their house—Mr. Cross roaring, his wife's placating screeches, their son's terrified shrieks. "Old man Cross's walloping his family," Freddie said.

"Tough bananas, hard to chew," Art said.

"Mind your own business," our mother said. "Go get ready for bed now, you stay up too late for school nights."

"Does Mr. Cross beat up his wife and kid?" I asked my father. He looked away from me before he spoke, as if he was checking the exact nature of the sounds coming from across the street.

"It takes all kinds," my father said. "Let's just say it's a heated dispute of a domestic quality, shall we? If that's not over your head. Now get to bed like your mother told you. Scoot!"

"Dope!" my brother Art said as we lay in our beds.

"You think he's gonna tell you anything the truth about that stuff?" Freddie said to me.

Clarence Hale Cross's mother was less dramatic. For the most part, she was a large shadow figure moving about their house, glimpsed through the windows, dressed always in what we called a housecoat (something my mother wore only when she cleaned or cooked our late Sunday breakfasts). I had a sense of her hovering, looking out often to check on her son's presence, his welfare. She emerged each evening to call him home to eat, and, donning a coat as worn and shapeless as her dress, though still shod in flapping slippers, each Saturday morning she walked to the A&P on Farewell Avenue, five blocks away, to shop for their groceries.

She returned, walking as slowly and wearily as a tired circus bear forced to dance too long on its hind legs, carrying two stuffed shopping bags, moving as if each step were her last. "Clarence Hale Cross!" she shouted in the big voice her son said came of the opera. "Come help Mother! Clarence Hale Cross, come help Mother now!"

Lie-A-Fornia

"I gotta go," Lie-A-Fornia said. We were on my porch, my mother for some reason there with us. "She broke her leg in a motorcycle accident racing in a ladies' race down in Baja California when we lived there before we moved here," he said.

"You said you lived in the Sierra Nevada!" I said.

"Poor thing," my mother said without thinking he heard, watching Mrs. Cross plod imperceptibly closer.

"Before that," he said to me. To my mother, Lie-A-Fornia said, "That's why she can't dance ballet anymore, her leg broke when she ran into this other motorcycle with hers, otherwise she'd still be a dancer in ballet. She was really good." Then he was gone, off our porch, down the street to help his mother bring their groceries home.

"More damn bull," I said.

"Hush your mouth," my mother said to me. "People will tell you all sorts of things. That's no reason to talk mean about any living soul. I don't approve of hearing vulgarity in any case."

I still wonder, after more than forty years, that we were no more cruel to him than we were. We called him names, *Lie-A-Fornia, BS-artist, liar-face,* threatened to take his pants off and play keep-away with them until he told the truth, teased him about his parents, caught him in his countless contradictory revisions of the stories he made up on the spot—but, though Art and Freddie were tough characters for their ages, and even I got in fistfights in our neighborhood and at school in an attempt to come up to their standards, we never physically picked on him.

That is no wonder, in part since he was so small for ten, pale, spindly, and wore glasses; we were not self-conscious bullies. It was in part also that he never confronted, never took up the repeated challenges we made to his honesty. And in part, I think some forty years after the fact, we must have enjoyed it to some extent—the sheer unbelievability of his assertions, his agility in his efforts to cover one lie with another, usually greater one, his seeming confidence and satisfaction in the excess of it all.

If we admired or respected anything about Clarence Hale Cross, however, it was his peculiar success at school with Miss Erna Haas, my teacher, a humorless spinster—perhaps sixty?—but not so dignified as to prevent her grabbing a back-sasser by his shirt and shaking him violently into a state of dizzied conformity.

The truth was, Lie-A-Fornia knew things.

We, my brothers and I, everyone else in our classes, our neighborhood, shared the communally obligatory stance of detesting and being bored by everything to do with school at Hartford Elementary except gym class, where we were permitted to play Dodge-ball, and recess, where we organized a rougher version of it called pull-away. Torn clothing and raw asphalt burns were badges we wore with disdain. Lie-A-Fornia, of course, never played pull-away; he huddled, as I remember, near the big double doors, waiting for the bell to end recess. I wonder now if he felt excluded, or if he spent the time thinking of all the things he knew, immersed in half-factual, half-fanciful information more interesting, exciting, absorbing, enriching, than schoolyard games.

For Clarence Hale Cross knew things. If Miss Erna Haas mentioned the Nobel Prize, he raised his hand, told us all about dynamite; when she spoke of President Roosevelt, he told us, his voice in a rush, about the man's death by massive stroke, that FDR's coffin was closed because his face was so horribly distorted by the final agony; told us Harry Truman was a haberdasher and long-time member of the corrupt Pendergast machine; when Miss Erna Haas taught our science book's chapter on reptiles (all I remember is they are cold-blooded, and only four poisonous reptiles live in North America), Clarence Hale Cross stood at his desk to deliver a semicoherent lecture on the spitting cobra's venom that blinded its prey; this led him to an association with the archer fish, which stuck its head above the pond's surface to bring down flies with a stream of water as accurate as anti-aircraft, which reminded him of German flak, which made him think of the Battle of the Bulge; when he was about to go to the blackboard to chalk a diagram illustrating how the Nazis perpetually reinforced their battle lines by regrouping and re-equipping scattered units, Miss Erna Haas finally stopped him, thanked him, and asked him to take his seat, please.

I could see no order, no system to what he knew—nor any purpose in the knowing. His knowledge, like his lies, was a kind of reservoir on the brink of overflow, and when our teacher, however inadvertently, tapped it, it sprang forth like a rift in a dike, a release that seemed to both ease and delight him. When his hand shot up, when he jumped to his feet, scattering his book, papers, and pencil to the floor, I saw a kind of light come into the bleary eyes behind his metal-framed spectacles, a spark of animated intensity flashed, vigor and joy glowed from his sallow face, in his puny frame.

"Washington, D.C., our nation's capital," he blurted, "got burned up by the redcoats in the War of 1812! Dolly Madison, the president's wife, saved all the important papers from the fire! She had pretty skin so she wore a mask on sunny days to keep it white. The war was already over but nobody knew it because they didn't have any telephones so they fought the Battle of New Orleans when they didn't even have to. . . ."

"Thank you very much, Clarence!" Miss Erna Haas said loudly to interrupt. "That's very nice, and we appreciate it. Now let's talk about what we read about the Supreme Court. Class? Please take your seat, Clarence, I'll call on you when I wish you to speak to us."

I think Miss Erna Haas saw it also—this life that came into

him when he told us things he knew. I saw this in her expression, a hint of a smile at the corners of her pinched, spinster's lips, a pleased bewilderment in her small eyes, magnified by the thick glasses she attached to her narrow bosom with a bright ribbon. I doubt anyone else in the fifth grade at Hartford Elementary, more than forty years ago, sensed this. When he spoke this way, our classmates sat stunned, as if burdened with an unbearable weight of ignorance and awe—and when he was, sooner or later, silenced by Miss Erna Haas, they shuffled their shoes under their desks and coughed, as if embarrassed or ashamed for us all.

"Miss Haas," I once asked after he talked about Englishmen cooking live peacocks for their dinner, "do you think that's all true? They cooked them while they were still alive?"

"Whether or not, it's surely very disturbing to know," she said. "Clarence is very unusually informed, aren't you, Clarence?"

"On some stuff," Lie-A-Fornia said.

I tried to explain it to Art and Freddie, seventh and eighth graders, but was unable to convey exactly what I meant. They thought nothing of it. "Big dealie wheelie," Art said.

"What a twerp! Why don't you guys just de-pants the little liar-twerp once!"

While it seemed so wondrous to me then, that he knew things, it is, now, so ordinary. Clarence Hale Cross read books. It amazes me, now, looking back, both that the source of his knowledge was so palpably mundane, and that I could not see the connection, the cause and effect, then.

Of course, we did not read, me, my brothers, our neighborhood friends. Reading was something of school, difficult, tedious, inflicted by our teachers. Miss Erna Haas required oral book reports, so I read about the Hardy Boys, the sports novels of John R. Tunis, and one book about an Irish setter, *Big Red*, that I actually liked. My mother read *McCall's* and *Saturday*

Evening Post; my father read *The Milwaukee Journal* each night before supper, gave us the Green Sheet insert Art and Freddie and I fought over for the comics and early box scores. Why should we read when we had radio serials, "Jack Armstrong," and "Your FBI in Peace and War" and "Inner Sanctum" and "The Shadow"? Our parents followed "One Man's Family," laughed at "Mr. Anthony" for the crazy people who came on the program to air ridiculous personal problems he solved with sage advice, and tested themselves against "Dr. I.Q."

And we had our neighborhood friends. We had Peggy-on-the-Bounce and Strikeout, played with a tennis ball against concrete steps or a brick wall. We had Washington Pole and Capture-the-Flag. Our father put up a basketball hoop, bought us one of the first vulcanized rubber balls for outdoor play in all weather. We had the pool at Gordon Park. We had our father's Raleigh cigarettes that Art stole, and Freddie taught us to smoke. Fads caught and held us like narcotics—yo-yo's once, boomerangs another time, placing pennies on the streetcar tracks, accumulating the flattened discs.

We had friends: Paul Hunt who dove into the shallow end of Gordon Park pool and spent the rest of his life from age twelve in an iron lung; Tommy Gorecki, who really was a grandnephew of the stripper Gilda Gray; Jack Crewson, whose older brother kept homing pigeons on their garage roof; Daniel Davies, who had only one testicle he would show on request; Jon Vos, who stole our first beer from the cases of Pabst his father bought at discount from the brewery downtown where he worked—more, others, but so few of their names come back to me, it has been so long.

And for a tinge of danger, excitement in our lives, there were the Italian boys of Victor Berger School we challenged and fought, beat and lost to in fights that blacked eyes and bloodied noses, split lips and chipped teeth, gashed knuckles. The swarthy Victor Berger boys scared me, but I fought them to satisfy my brothers and our friends from Locust Street and Hartford Elementary.

Lie-A-Fornia had none of these, no games, no fad-toys, could not and would not fight, no friends. Lie-A-Fornia had books.

And just now I remember, going once to the East Side Branch of the Milwaukee Public Library, on Prospect Place, a dozen blocks from home—I do not recall why I should have gone there, early in the spring evening. Prospect was a noisy, busy artery, autos honking impatiently at the four-way stop signs, streetcars rattling and screeching on their tracks, sparks spitting from the overhead booms powering them, the Oriental Theater and Bowling Lanes, a White Tower hamburger shop always too crowded to find a counter stool free. I entered the East-Side Branch of the Milwaukee Public Library, and it was bright with fluorescents and quiet. It smelled of dust, empty except for a seedy woman at a check-out desk and Clarence Hall Cross, alone at one of the long tables, surrounded by books, reading. I remember how loud my voice sounded in the tiny neighborhood library, though I knew to whisper when I spoke. "The hell you doing?" I said. He looked over his book at me, blinked his eyes behind his glasses, squinted.

"I'm studying up to write a whole book on how we can make enough electricity for the whole world if they build a dam like Boulder on the Amazon River in Africa."

"Let's see," I said, and took the book from his hands, read the spine. It was a pictorial history of military aviation during what was called The Great War when it was published.

"Liar," I said to him.

"Not this one," he said. "This I'm reading because I think later I'll study how to design cars and planes. These," he said, reaching out both his hands to touch the volumes arrayed about him like a low, half-finished wall.

"Lie like a rug, Lie-A-Fornia," I said. There was a book of political cartoons, one on a day in the life of a Chinese boy named Chin, *Roget's Thesaurus,* Brady's Civil War photographs, Jack London's *Martin Eden, A Hundred and One Famous Poems* (a long, thin book with a picture of each poet set in an oval above each poem), a book on beekeeping for beginners, others I cannot remember.

"I read the one story by Jack London Haas made us," I said.

"I read everything he ever wrote, some twice," he said. "Once he lived with cannibals and had to eat part of a person with them," he said. "He said it tastes like pig, which is what they call it, long pig," he said.

"Tell me another one," I said, "and I might just even believe you." I gave him back his cartoons. "I'm going to the five-and-dime," I said. "Come on, we can try and swipe something."

"I would except I can't," Lie-A-Fornia said. "My dad's coming to get me. We're gonna bowl at Oriental and then go have dinner at the Pfister Hotel and see the ice show."

"Baloney sausage," I told him, and left—the Oriental did not permit children to bowl their lanes, the Pfister was the most expensive hotel in Milwaukee, the Ice Capades only came to the city in winter. If Mr. Cross was anywhere in the vicinity, it would be the Murray Elbow Room, if he was not at work for the Milwaukee Road, tending his garden, or drinking at Bette & Dad's Tavern.

I left him there with his grab bag of strange books, in the fluorescent brightness and utter quiet that smelled of dust, with his lies and all he knew, and went out on Prospect Place, perhaps to shoplift something at Woolworth's or the nearby hardware store, I do not remember now.

He moved to our neighborhood from California—a far, exotic place then—but where, when Mrs. Cross died suddenly, he and his father moved away to, I have no idea. In memory, it feels to me as if Lie-A-Fornia lived a long time with us on Locust Street—years—but it was less than a year, the spring semester of school, most of the following summer. I cannot explain this temporal distortion in my thinking. The facts are simply that Clarence Hale Cross came to us from California, was my fifth-grade classmate at Hartford Elementary for one semester, lived across the street from me, summer vacation began, autumn neared, and then his mother died, and he and his father were gone forever.

It was twilight, when nothing is quite clearly seen in the summer haze. Suddenly there was a long white ambulance across the street; it maneuvered, backed up across the curb to the porch of Lie-A-Fornia's house. We gathered, as close as we dared, watched the two men wearing white carry the stretcher out, down the porch steps, roll it into the back of the ambulance—I stood on my tiptoes to see over Freddie's head. "Is it his old man?" I asked.

"Can't tell," Art said, "it's all covered."

"Pretty slick," Freddie said of the gleaming ambulance, its mirroring chrome, the dome light rotating, casting a pale rosy wash over us, the metallic smack of the doors shutting.

"Move out the way, you little farts," the driver said before he started his engine. We stepped back, watched the ambulance bump down over the curb, turn, and accelerate away—I had one brief look through the side window at the covered form on the stretcher, crossed leather straps holding the blanket in place.

"It could be either," Art said.

"It's too small for his old man. It's gotta be his ma," Freddie said.

"It's too big for sure for Lie-A-Fornia," I said. We waited a long time, sat on our porch watching Lie-A-Fornia's house; lights came on inside as night fell, but the curtains were drawn —we could not even see shadow-shapes moving within.

"Get inside. You're morbid, the three of you," our mother said. I never learned for certain if Lie-A-Fornia was home when his mother died. For all I know, he might have been at the branch public library all the while we watched her body carried out and into the ambulance. We did not see him again until her graveside funeral service at Roselawn.

Our father read the curt obituary in the *Journal* aloud to us, the notice of the service. "Do we have to?" Freddie asked.

"Of course you have to," our mother said. "He's your friend, and he's lost his mother, poor thing, you owe him common decency."

"He's not my friend," Art said.

"He's a fellow human being," she said, "and so was his mother, poor thing."

Mrs. Cross's age was given in the obituary. When I asked my father if forty-six was young to die, he said, "On the average, yes. You're best off not to worry about it. Live your life and be happy," he said. To our mother, he said Mrs. Cross was by no means a spring chicken when she gave birth to her son; my mother asked him what that had to do with the price of bananas.

I had never been to a cemetery; all my grandparents were buried in Indiana, where my parents lived before they moved to Milwaukee. Roselawn was on the west side of town, a long ride. A marble orchard, my father called it; Freddie called it a bone-yard. Our mother shushed them. We parked, had a long walk to the graveside. I was awed by the stones we passed, tried to read names and dates, calculate life spans, felt the odd contradiction of so much mute granite, its inherent silence broken by song-birds, the hot summer breeze, the sound my shoes made in the thick green grass. "Walk between, don't step on none," Art whispered to me as we followed Freddie and our parents.

Of the service I remember the man who spoke, his white collar, but not his words. The full sun reflecting off the coffin's ornaments hurt my eyes. The fresh-dug earth was mounded beneath a green carpet less green than the grass. There was a canopy erected, its edges flapping softly in the wind. Besides my family, there were only Miss Erna Haas and old Mrs. Konecky, who lived two houses down from ours on Locust Street. Miss Erna Haas stood the entire time with an embroidered hankie pressed to her nose, as if something smelled bad. My father stood like a soldier at ease, hands clasped behind his back, staring out across the open grave, as though he studied cloud formations. My mother sniffed and sighed. Art and Freddie fidgeted.

I watched Lie-A-Fornia and his father. It was very strange to see Mr. Cross in a dark, double-breasted suit, white shirt and tie, vest, shined shoes. His hair glistened with tonic, plastered close to his head, unruffled by gusts. His hands closed in fists at his sides, sweat trailed along his razor-burned jaws, gathered in the creases of his neck. He cleared his throat often, as if he meant to turn away and spit.

Clarence Hale Cross did not weep. His suit was a light blue, flannel, too heavy for summer. Arms limp at his sides, he clenched and unclenched his hands, otherwise only looked straight ahead, but not as if he saw anything. I watched his eyes behind his glasses to see if he cried, but he only blinked, squinted now and again against the sharp light. I wondered what he thought.

I wondered if he kept from tears for his mother by thinking of all the things he knew, if he evaded his grief by filling the whole of his being with a rush of facts and fancies and monstrous hybrids so rich there was no seam in it, no breach for his loss and hurt to invade and touch him. Or did he think only of his mother, force himself to remember her in life with such detailed precision that she might seem still alive to him, given a kind of life by the sheer insistence of his imagining—and so not dead, truly, about to be buried, and so no weeping called for?

The service for Mrs. Cross probably did not last as long as I felt, then, it had. Our father led the way, shook Mr. Cross's hand, said, "Condolences."

Mr. Cross nodded. "Heart," he said.

"Oh, I am so very sorry!" our mother said to him.

"Heart, you know," he replied. I was too busy trying to plan what to say and do to hear what my brothers said.

I said to Mr. Cross, "Sorry Mrs. Cross died." He said nothing to me, but took my hand; his was hard and rough on mine, but gentle, as if he feared he might accidentally crush it. To Lie-A-Fornia I was able to say only, "Sorry." His small hand was moist and warm, and I held it carefully, as if it might scorch me.

"Thanks," is what he said to me—I think I expected him to begin some ludicrous story, about the cause of his mother's death, where he had been in the days since she died. Out of sight, on our walk back to our 1941 Plymouth, I rubbed my hand raw-dry on my best pair of trousers.

I suppose a few weeks passed before Clarence Hale Cross and his father moved away from Locust Street. I saw him, spoke with him less often than usual after the funeral—three, four times? Those weeks seemed to pass so quickly, summer ending, and then they were gone forever, so absolutely and totally not there, as though they had never been.

That is how, now, looking back, all the times and people of my life since then seem—gone, wholly and irrevocably, the sum and span of my life a kind of ill-shaped, half-formed void too insubstantial to declare itself or its meaning to me. If I have attained to any wisdom, it is that time is the one true profundity; it is recoverable, retainable—one's life—for the most part only in abstractions. Names. Dates. Of interest and significance—my life—to me alone.

Mr. Cross and his son left, summer ended, school began, time raced. In time, my brothers and I went our ways, found work and marriages, homes, children, the normative complements of merely sufficient time. Our parents died. My brother Art died—killed in a commonplace auto accident. The wife of one of Freddie's sons died recently, cancer—we live a thousand miles apart.

I contend we all have—had—good lives, comfortable if not affluent, secure if not untouched, satisfying though unspectacular. A husband and father, soon to be a grandfather, I seldom wish I had done anything differently, know too well such speculation is idle, feckless, frustrating.

Names and dates. Minor successes and small failures. Contentment leavened by occasional joy, no more than a fair portion of disappointment. Little despair and no deep or lasting regret. I have not earned a lament, expect a conventional eulogy.

"So why you moving away?" I asked Lie-A-Fornia.

"My dad hates the railroad industry so he's bought us a ranch in Montana we're gonna raise ostriches you can ride like a horse and they make boots from their skin," he said once.

"Alaska," he said another time, "my dad's got this lodge you can trap furs and shoot moose and bears all year around." Liar, I called him.

"Florida," he said yet another time. "We're building this-here sailing schooner clipper ship and sailing around the world at the equator it'll take two years probably, so I won't be in school. I'll have to study on my own. We'll eat sharks and whatever we catch, squids and eels even."

Montana, Alaska, Florida, all the world's seas and oceans, the Kingdom of Arabia where Mr. Cross would prospect for oil, his son would own a camel, Haiti, French Indo-China, a fishing village in Wales, a diamond mine in South Africa, the salt flats of Utah, skiing in Vermont, Cairo, Paris, New Orleans, pack mules in Wyoming, the unexplored interior of Brazil, where naked savages armed with blowguns sought your head for shrinking, wheat acreage in Kansas, a Finger Lakes vineyard—

the four corners of the earth, Timbuktu, Shangri-la, Ultima Thule, the Mountains of the Moon. I called him a liar.

Where did you go, Lie-A-Fornia? And what did you make of all you knew and dreamed? Did you ever cease telling your lies to anyone who listened? Did you never learn to speak such truths as others wish and need to hear?

And, oh, Lie-A-Fornia, I do wish I could tell you how, when I remember you—clear, exact, tangible among all the abstractions—I so wish I had learned what you might have taught me.

These stories, since revised, appeared originally in the following fora:

"Fearing What Dreams?" *New England Review* 3, no. 3, 1981.

"The American Dream: The Book of Boggs," *Square One* 2, 1985; reprinted in *Kansas Quarterly* 19, no. 3, 1987; reprinted in *Best of the West II*, 1989; reprinted as "The Lord and T. Bone Boggs," in *Oklahoma Today* 43, no. 4, 1993.

"Poet-In-Residence," *TWA Ambassador* 19, no. 2, 1986.

"Immediate Review," *TWA Ambassador* 19, no. 5, 1986.

"Bunce's Neighbors," *Witness* 1, no. 2, 1987.

"Elegy for Orrin Bodine II," *Ellipsis*, 1988.

"The Apotheosis of Neddie Hacke," *St. Andrews Review*, no. 36, 1989.

"Batteiger's Muse," *Manoa* 3, no. 1, 1991.

"The Way You Know in Dreams," *New England Review*, nos. 3–4, 1991.

"Modern History," *Nimrod* 35, no. 1, 1991.

"Lie-A-Fornia" (originally titled "The Great Liar"), *Oklahoma Today* 42, no. 4, 1992.